Do The Right Thing

Storytelling Secrets of Five Screenplays That Embrace Diversity

Karla R. Fuller

MICHAEL WIESE PRODUCTIONS

Published by Michael Wiese Productions
12400 Ventura Blvd. #1111
Studio City, CA 91604
(818) 379-8799, (818) 986-3408 (FAX)
mw@mwp.com
www.mwp.com

Cover design by Johnny Ink
Copyediting by Karen Krumpak

Manufactured in the United States of America
Copyright © 2022 by Karla R. Fuller
First Printing 2022

Library of Congress Cataloging-in-Publication Data Names: Fuller, Karla Rae, author.
Title: Do the write thing! : storytelling secrets of five screenplays that embrace diversity / Karla R. Fuller.
Description: Studio City, CA : Michael Wiese Productions, [2022]. | Summary: "Do The Write Thing! offers screenwriting strategies that focus on diversity, equity and inclusion The goal is to teach an already challenging writing mode that requires screenwriters to create complex human experiences through visual storytelling. We are in a critical historical moment where the importance of screenwriting can be of the utmost usefulness in the observation of racism, inequity and inclusion in all media. The screen representations of race, ethnicity, gender, sexuality or class are not often explicitly addressed at the "front end" of the film production process, specifically, during the creation of the screenplay (whether original or adapted from outside source material). The idea is to introduce and reinforce the importance of accountability for what you write for the screen. This is not to limit the screenwriter's creative impulses, but rather to create and engage them in consistent ways that reveal unconscious biases and instances of systemic racism. We will use five case studies of commercially successful and award-winning screenplays that resist stereotypes to present multidimensional depictions of historically underrepresented groups, such as LGBTQ, African American, Latino and Asian American. In the discussions of each individual screenplay issues such as the adaptation process, plot structure and devices, characterization, setting, symbolism, and genre conventions are introduced and analyzed in depth"-- Provided by publisher.
Identifiers: LCCN 2021045698 | ISBN 9781615933402 (trade paperback)
Subjects: LCSH: Motion picture plays--Case studies. | Social justice.
Classification: LCC PN1996 .F85 2022 | DDC 808.2/3--dc23/eng/20220113
LC record available at https://lccn.loc.gov/2021045698

"It is better to light a candle than curse the darkness."

— Chinese Proverb

Table of Contents

ACKNOWLEDGMENTS

If Michael Wiese had not invited me to do a book project with his publishing company, this book would not exist. We go back a long way. Thank you, Michael, for this fantastic opportunity.

I am also grateful to my dear friends, Julie Sandor and Barbara Selznick, who took time away from their busy lives and beautiful families to read early drafts of each chapter and give me much needed feedback. I will be forever in your debt, my true-blue friends!

And finally, my family: Gladys Fuller, Nancy McDaniel, and Tara and Ivan Lamourt.

Thank you for believing in me and encouraging me to do what I ask others to do: write!

FOREWORD

In *Do the Right Thing: Storytelling Secrets of Five Screenplays that Embrace Diversity*, Karla R. Fuller offers a north star, a beacon of hope for screenwriters in search of affirmation that their stories of diversity and intersectionality have artistic and commercial value. Fuller serves as knowledgeable guide, meticulously analyzing each screenplay in order to help screenwriters navigate the often terrifying terrain of the blank page, as well as encouraging friend, instilling the belief that in understanding these case studies, they, too, can take creative risks and honor stories that challenge the singular narrative. Thus, *Do the Right Thing* is a roadmap, especially for screenwriters from historically underrepresented backgrounds, to boldly pursue the writing of stories that reflect their everyday lived experiences. This book is essential to any screenwriter's arsenal of tools and underscores a changing film and TV landscape that is finally catching up to what many of us already knew: that diverse, personal, and complex narratives are good for the business of entertainment — and for our collective culture as a whole.

— Thavary Krouch (Independent Film Coordinator
for the Chicago Film Office)

"The single story creates stereotypes, and the problem with stereotypes is not that they are untrue, but that they are incomplete. They make one story become the only story . . . When we reject the single story, when we realize there is never a single story about any place, we regain a kind of paradise."

— Chimamanda Ngozi Adichie,
"The Danger of a Single Story"

Doing the Right Thing

A Changing Industry

How does an emerging writer break through with a feature script that reflects a multicultural world? Through this book, you will discover how complex, thoughtful choices made five recent screenplays into successful films — and the principles that screenwriters can use for similar results.

The criteria for choosing these specific five films rests in part on these scripts as a group being representative of recent film projects that in some way advance a counternarrative to mainstream filmmaking, with its all-too-often stereotypical and one-dimensional characterizations. Films with a lot of buzz such as *Crazy Rich Asians* and *Black Panther*, both released in 2018, were mainly noted for their diversity primarily in terms of racial representation. However, because of their status as mega-budget narratives, they are by necessity crafted with the largest possible audience in mind to cover their massive budgets. These types of mega films rarely, if ever, offer highly personal narratives that capture underrepresented perspectives that take us beyond the simple appearance of racial diversity. Their big-money studio business model, at the end of the day, ultimately helps reinforce the status quo. The cinematic narratives chosen for this book prove that many different dimensions, not just age or race or gender or sexuality, make a person who they are. Characters need to be relatable, which doesn't mean predictable or even necessarily always sympathetic — oftentimes a big misunderstanding of many beginning screenwriters.

Crafting a compelling screenplay that reflects diversity, equity, and inclusion can pay off commercially as well as artistically. Changing demographics of U.S. movie audiences suggest the more diversity — the more success! Nearly 50 percent of frequent moviegoers are nonwhite, according to the Motion Picture Association (MPA) 2019 THEME Report.[1] Mass media has to appeal to a more colorful audience, an audience with a mix of races, ethnicities, genders, sexualities, and countless untold stories.

This book is guided by specific foundational ideas — goals and actions you can take to "liberate" your screenplay from clichéd and formulaic approaches:

- Thinking about the meaning in the message of your screenplay. In other words, does it contribute positively to a more inclusive worldview rather than repeat familiar tropes that reinforce current social hierarchies and systems?
- Avoiding stereotypical depictions (dangerous black men; feisty, hypersexualized black and Latinx women; perpetually foreign, one-dimensional, or "model minority" Asian Americans).
- Revealing systemic racism through human stories.
- Remembering the interconnectedness of all human life and the multiple identities that impact your own work.[2]

I have selected five screenplays that have broken barriers and defined success in the U.S. film industry for analysis in this book. These screenplays have given voice to those underrepresented

---

[1] Motion Picture Association, "2019 THEME Report," accessed February 4, 2022, https://www.motionpictures.org/wp-content/uploads/2020/03/MPA-THEME-2019.pdf.

[2] Alan Jenkins, "Action! Ten Things Hollywood Can Do to Fight Racism and Promote Justice," LinkedIn, June 4, 2020, https://www.linkedin.com/pulse/action-ten-things-hollywood-can-do-fight-racism-promote-alan-jenkins/.

narratives, depicting characters who are fresh, multidimensional, and overwhelmingly relatable through very specific human experiences. Whether expanding a genre, as in *Get Out*, or working within a well-established three act structure, like *Moonlight*, these five films are all remarkable for their unprecedented audacity in offering us fully formed worlds that counteract historically stereotypical characters and overly predictable storytelling.

In Chapter One, *Moonlight* (2016) depicts the drama of a young African American man at three pivotal points in his life, as a child, a teenager, and a young adult. The leading character contends with an unstable homelife, a dangerous neighborhood, and a burgeoning sexuality. In the end, he returns to an authentic self with the help of his first and only lover. *Moonlight* won Academy Awards for Best Picture and Best Adapted Screenplay.

Chapter Two focuses on *Get Out* (2017), a horror film about a young African American who visits his white girlfriend's seemingly politically liberal parents for the weekend. But during the weekend, a terrifying plan to auction off his body and soul to the highest bidder is shockingly revealed in ways reminiscent of the U.S. slave trade. The film won an Academy Award for Best Original Screenplay.

In *Mudbound* (2017), the film in Chapter Three, two men return home from World War II to work on a farm in rural Mississippi, where they struggle to deal with racism and adjusting to life after war. One white, one black, they form a dangerous bond of friendship that threatens their very lives and the lives of each of their families. The film was nominated for four Academy Awards, including Best Adapted Screenplay by Dee Rees and Virgil Williams, making director Dee Rees the first African American woman to be nominated for Best Adapted Screenplay.

Chapter Four's *Roma* (2018) recounts a year in the life of a maid for a middle-class family in Mexico City in the early 1970s. Based on the memories of writer/director Alfonso Cuarón, the character of the maid is foregrounded as both the victim and savior of this troubled family. The film won Academy Awards for Best Director and Best

International Film (a first for a Mexican film) and was nominated for Best Original Screenplay.

Always Be My Maybe (2019), available to most viewers only on Netflix, is the subject of Chapter Five. This rom-com tells the story of Asian Americans Sasha and Marcus, who met as children and grew up together, and whom everyone assumed would wind up together except them. When they reconnect fifteen years later, sparks fly between them, Sasha now a celebrity chef and Marcus a working-class contractor at his father's company. But the differences in their professional success threaten to pull them apart until they each learn that mutual support, love, and family is what matters most. *Variety* reported that the film was viewed by 32 million households in its first four weeks of release.[3]

There is a new awareness of how diverse film content can be and how audiences positively receive all well-crafted work — an awareness that defies traditional expectations and assumptions. And the emergence of "new" studios such as Netflix is shaking up the game with diverse content. In other words, all five films, given their specialized subject matter or small scale — *Roma*, with its focus on an indigenous maid character, the treatment of controversial themes such as same-sex romantic relationships in *Moonlight*, the use of satire in *Get Out*, the rare attention paid to working class Asian American characters in *Always Be My Maybe*, and the so-called less commercial period genre of historical fiction in *Mudbound* — would be expected to attract very small audiences. According to the MPA 2019 Annual THEME Report, home and mobile entertainment, which includes streaming services, grew by 14 percent worldwide from the previous year.[4] Once only a small part of the business, the streaming industry continues to transform content with its growing numbers and increasing budgets. Indeed, that same report announced that as of January 2019, Netflix had become a member of the MPA, the only

[3] Janko Roettgers, "'The Perfect Date,' 'Always Be My Maybe' Draw Big Crowds on Netflix," *Variety*, July 17, 2019, https://variety.com/2019/digital/news/the-perfect-date-always-be-my-maybe-draw-big-crowds-on-netflix-1203270482/.

[4] "2019 THEME Report."

streaming service to do so in the MPA's nearly one-hundred-year history.[5] The fact that three of the five films discussed here (*Mudbound*, *Roma*, and *Always Be My Maybe*) were produced and distributed by Netflix affirms that projects embracing diversity are being supported by this new and thriving sector of the industry.

Further, the Academy of Motion Pictures Arts and Sciences instituted in 2021 a set of requirements for films to qualify for the Best Picture Oscar, with the sole goal of increasing diversity, equity, and inclusion in future films. Academy President David Rubin and Academy CEO Dawn Hudson said in a joint statement: "The aperture must widen to reflect our diverse global population in both the creation of motion pictures and in the audiences who connect with them. The Academy is committed to playing a vital role in helping make this a reality."[6]

This book does not focus on tips so much as exploring stories in a way that will hopefully help you expand your understanding of stories — both your own and the stories of others — and help you tell more complex stories. It is not intended to reinforce a restrictive notion of identity politics that dampens the creative spark or suggests who can tell which stories. Our five examples are diverse in a number of significant ways. These films offer not only diversity in terms of the expected on-screen representation of underrepresented identities (i.e., queer, African American, Latino, Asian American), but also in terms of genre and their diversely populated screenwriting creative teams. Each film offers a different genre: LGBTQ drama in *Moonlight*, horror in *Get Out*, historical drama in *Mudbound*, international drama in *Roma*, and rom-com antics in *Always Be My Maybe*. Their successes demonstrate not prescriptive limitations but room for exponentially more creative storytelling. As will become clear (if it's not already), meaningful and inclusive collaboration produces great films.

---

[5] "2019 THEME Report."
[6] Oscars, "Academy Establishes Representation and Inclusion Standards for Oscars Eligibility," September 8, 2020, https://www.oscars.org/news/academy-establishes-representation-and-inclusion-standards-oscarsr-eligibility.

CHAPTER ONE

A
Different
Shade
of
Love

in *MOONLIGHT* (2016)

"I thought five people would see this film: my mom, my sister, and maybe a few close friends. The fact that it's playing in one theater is a privilege . . . Nothing we did was geared toward making the movie fit this box or that box. There's something to be said about how the film can create the market, and create the campaign."

— Barry Jenkins, director
and co-writer of *Moonlight*

Writer/director Barry Jenkins' words in the quote above resonate with so many filmmakers who have an urgent story to tell but aren't sure that there is an audience waiting to see their work, their labor of love. I am struck by Jenkins' humility in his expression of awe at the prospect of his film showing in even one theater. And yet, he follows with the declaration that maybe, just maybe, a film itself can create the "market," and more directly can specifically produce an audience without checking off "this box or that box" of a common set of expectations in the mainstream movie industry.

Barry Jenkins grew up in the economically disadvantaged Liberty City neighborhood of Miami, Florida. He did not know his father, and his mother struggled with drug addiction. In high school he was a talented athlete who ran track and played football. He attended Florida State University as an English major before changing to film by enrolling in the university's College of Motion Picture Arts, earning a Bachelor of Fine Arts degree in 2003. Then Jenkins moved to Los Angeles to make films. He worked as a production assistant at Oprah Winfrey's Harpo Studios. In 2007 he moved again, this time to San Francisco, hoping to make his own movie. Jenkins made his debut feature, *Medicine for Melancholy*, in 2008 while working at a Banana Republic retail store. Though made on an extremely small budget, *Medicine for Melancholy* was well received by critics who felt that the film, which "describes 24 hours in a budding romance between two young people in a gentrifying San Francisco," effectively "raised issues in a spirit of exploration rather than didacticism."[1]

While working as a carpenter, Jenkins pursued two projects that ultimately went nowhere. One of them was based on the 1974 James Baldwin novel *If Beale Street Could Talk*, which was eventually made after *Moonlight*, but he didn't have the rights at that time. Then a mutual friend of playwright Tarell Alvin McCraney gave Jenkins a script that was set in the same place and same time that Jenkins had grown up in. The film that resulted was *Moonlight*, which Jenkins described as a "hood-arthouse coming-of-age LGBT drama" that dramatizes three points in the main character's life, as a child, then teenager, then young adult.[2]

As it happens, *Moonlight* did play in just one theater (on one screen) for many weeks, but that wasn't the end of the film's performance. What Jenkins' quote doesn't reveal is the fact that this film

---

[1] Patricia Bauer, "Barry Jenkins," *Encyclopedia Britannica*, accessed October 31, 2021, https://www.britannica.com/biography/Barry-Jenkins.
[2] Bauer, "Barry Jenkins."

grew from one screen to four screens, and gradually all the way up to over fifteen hundred. On a budget of $1.5 million,[3] *Moonlight's* box office gross totaled $27 million domestically (in the United States, Canada, and Puerto Rico) and, even more remarkable, $65 million worldwide.[4] It won Academy Awards for Best Picture, Best Supporting Actor, and, most importantly for our purposes here, Best Adapted Screenplay by Barry Jenkins from the story in the unproduced play by Tarell Alvin McCraney.

McCraney's original title — "In Moonlight Black Boys Look Blue" — tells us an awful lot about the spirit and nature of this story, even though it wasn't used for the film. Moonlight, it suggests, has the power to transform a stereotypical appearance of blackness (and all the assumptions that go with it), of "Black Boys," to something more poetic and as deep as the color of the ocean, dark blue and filled with life.

In the film, our protagonist is given three names (Little, Chiron, and Black), none of which say much of anything about his inner life, his sense of self beyond visual appearances or how others name him. His story, his journey, reminds us that a character's inner life, where often their authentic wants and needs live, is the most important thing that they can bring to relationships. We see during the course of the film how our embattled protagonist navigates his world, filled with brief moments of love and caring yet also, much too often, neglect, fear, and a lack of love. But in the end, he has a serious reckoning with the authentic self that he (and we) thought might be permanently lost. And even if we don't know exactly what will happen after this brief reappearance of profound vulnerability and love, we know this: that all people, despite appearances to the contrary, have the need for love and deep connection.

---

[3] Barry Jenkins (@BarryJenkins), "Yes fellas by why on earth…," Twitter Post, February 28, 2018, 6:06 PM, https://twitter.com/barryjenkins/status/968985836439052288?lang=en.

[4] Box Office Mojo, "*Moonlight* – Box Office," IMDbPro, accessed February 8, 2022, https://pro.imdb.com/title/tt4975722/boxoffice.

SYNOPSIS

This story takes place in the Liberty City section of Miami in the 1980s at three different points in the protagonist's life, as a child, a teenager, and a young adult.

Part I. Little

A little boy runs away from a group of bullies who are out for blood — life or death. The boy runs into an abandoned crack house and waits until a man, Juan, comes in and rescues him after a bit of coaxing. Juan takes Little out to eat and notices how hungry he is. He tries to get the boy to talk but he is too busy eating. Juan then takes Little to spend the night at his home with his girlfriend Teresa. When he takes the boy back to his own home the next day, his mother, Paula, is very angry that he didn't tell her where he was.

Little starts spending more and more time with Juan, who teaches him how to swim, or at least to float on his back. They grow very close.

Little goes to Juan and Teresa's house. He expresses his hatred for his mother Paula, who is a drug addict, then asks Juan what a faggot is. After Juan explains, Little asks if he himself is one. He then asks Juan about his drug dealing and selling to his mother. Little leaves, and Juan appears tearfully remorseful.

Part II. Chiron

Little has turned into a teenaged boy going by the name Chiron who looks lonely and lost. He is attending high school, where he basically has only one friend, Kevin. Juan has long since passed away. Chiron is harassed at school by a punk named Terrel, who mocks Chiron in the middle of class until their teacher kicks Terrel out. Chiron is shown on his own, isolated and angry at his mother's ongoing drug addiction and at his classmates, who bully him even during class time. Kevin, who he's known since he was Little, shares with Chiron his sexual experiences with girls, which constantly keep him in trouble at school. Chiron has a dream about Kevin having sex from what he described and is disturbed by it.

One night, Chiron goes out to the beach at night for some peace and quiet. Suddenly, Kevin appears, seemingly out of nowhere. They talk honestly about their struggles and feelings, especially their dark ones. Kevin nicknames Chiron "Black," but when Chiron reacts negatively, Kevin innocently asks him, "Don't you like it?" This is the first time anyone has ever asked Chiron what he wishes to be called. Though Chiron simply responds by shrugging his shoulders, the boys discover a mutual attraction during their conversation, ending in a kiss and Kevin giving Chiron a hand job.

The next day at school Chiron attempts to talk with Kevin but is stopped by Terrel. Terrel, sensing a bond between Chiron and Kevin, sets them up in a violent game where Kevin is forced to hit Chiron until he stops getting back up from being knocked down. Chiron continues to get back up despite the blows, even though Kevin begs him to stay down. The next day, an enraged Chiron hits Terrel with a classroom chair so hard that he breaks it. Afterward, Chiron is taken away by the police.

Part III. Black

The story jumps forward about ten years. Chiron, now named Black, is living in Atlanta, Georgia. Black now dresses similar to Juan, and he has similarly become a drug dealer. He looks physically strong, with a muscular physique. Black taunts his criminal underlings with a cruel sense of humor that instills fear in them.

One night, Black receives an unexpected phone call from Kevin, who apologizes for what happened in high school and invites him back to Florida to visit where he works as a cook. On his way through Florida, Black visits his mom, who is in rehab and wants to make amends. Black accepts her apologies for not being a good mother to him. She further hopes that Black can learn to trust somebody despite all that he's been through.

When Black arrives in Florida, Kevin cooks him a special meal at the restaurant where he works. They go back to Kevin's apartment, where Kevin describes having a son that he is committed to raising and asks about Black's personal life. Black makes the admission that he has not let "nobody touch him" since that night on the beach with Kevin in high school. Shocked and saddened, Kevin takes Black in his arms and strokes his head gently as we return to an image of Little at the edge of the ocean.

The Universal from the Specific

Lorraine Hansberry, author of *A Raisin in the Sun* and the first African American female playwright to have a play produced on Broadway, is quoted as saying: "I believe that one of the most sound ideas in dramatic writing is that in order to create something universal, you must pay very great attention to the specific."[5] As stated earlier, Barry Jenkins described *Moonlight* as a "hood-arthouse coming-of-age LGBT drama." Whether he was partly joking or not, his attempt to place this very distinctive film within preset industry categories utterly fails. It fails because *Moonlight* doesn't speak to the unique mix of genres at play. The film does have elements of hood, arthouse, coming-of-age, and LGBT themes, but significantly those individual elements do not define it; the elements mix to create a completely exceptional story. At the same time, the many generic identifiers do tell us of some of the possible points of entry

[5] Lorraine Hansberry, "Lorraine Hansberry discusses her play 'A Raisin in the Sun,'" Studs Terkel Radio Archive, WFMT Radio, Chicago, IL: WFMT, May 12, 1959, https://studsterkel.wfmt.com/programs/lorraine-hansberry-discusses-her-play-raisin-sun.

for audiences — in other words, some of the qualities that make this film universal.

More so than classic Hollywood tradition, Jenkins has been strongly influenced by international filmmakers from Asia, Europe, and Latin America such as Hong Kong's Wong Kar-wai (*Chungking Express*, *In The Mood for Love*), Taiwan's Hou Hsiao-Hsien, France's Claire Denis, Scotland's Lynne Ramsey (*Ratcatcher*), and Argentina's Lucrecia Martel.[6] For example, according to Chris O'Falt of Indiewire, "The unique three-chapter approach Jenkins took in *Moonlight* was directly inspired by Hou's *Three Times*, in which three romances — stretching over 100 years — feature the same two actors."[7] Jenkins' international influences speak to an openness to different ways of not only viewing but also telling stories through acknowledging and celebrating both the specificity of cinematic experiences and the universality of emotion. O'Falt recounts:

> Just ask Jenkins, who saw Wong's *Chungking Express* as a young film student and was immediately captivated. "I'd never really seen a foreign film before; I wasn't watching a lot of foreign films," the *Moonlight* director recalled in a 2016 video for Criterion. "I remember just being sucked in, and having a feeling of how big the world was, but how small it was at the same time. Because I don't speak Mandarin or Cantonese, I'd never been outside of the state of Florida, and I'm watching this film, and I'm feeling all these things."[8]

Adaptation and Ownership

For playwright Tarell McCraney, the author of "In Moonlight Black Boys Look Blue," the inspiration behind this story is autobiographical. The characters of Chiron, his mother Paula, and father figure Juan are all based on McCraney's own life, family, friends, and

[6] Chris O'Falt, "Barry Jenkins' 'Moonlight': See the Seven Foreign Films That Inspired the Oscar Winner," IndieWire, May 31, 2017, https://www.indiewire.com/2017/05/barry-jenkins-film-style-wong-kar-wai-claire-denis-lynne-ramsay-1201834261/2/.
[7] O'Falt, "See the Seven Foreign Films."
[8] Tyler Aquilina, "Why you should dive into the work of Hong Kong director Wong Kar Wai," *Entertainment Weekly*, March 20, 2021, https://ew.com/movies/why-you-should-watch-films-of-wong-kar-wai/.

foes. In other words, the subject matter is completely personal and subjective.

McCraney thought about each aspect of the storytelling very carefully. For example, in an article for *Vice*, Monica Uszerowicz describes how choosing the name Chiron for the lead character was an intentional reference to the Chiron of Greek mythology:

> Chiron's name is no coincidence. Deemed the Wounded Healer by Carl Jung, Chiron the centaur is quite unlike his lusty brethren. The calm hero trains Hercules and, upon receiving a fatal wound that will never heal due to his inability to die, sacrifices his immortality, saving someone else. "There are parts of [Chiron] that will never heal," explains McCraney. "His job is to find ways to heal others. I think it's important, in understanding what we think of masculinity — especially in the black community — to consider that when we think of who's been hurt, we often remember how they callous over, not how they have ability to be generous."[9]

Though McCraney's story was originally conceived as a stage play, McCraney's friends believed it would make a great film and that it was inherently cinematic. He wrote it quickly and kept it short, resulting in just about sixty pages that "confronted his mother's decline, the brutality of the childhood bullying he experienced — he was hit with bricks, lost several teeth — as well of moments of grace he achieved with Blue (the real-life inspiration for the character Juan) and the transcendence of a solitary sexual encounter with his only true childhood friend."[10] When the play reached Barry Jenkins, it still needed a lot of work, but Jenkins has stated that he thought he knew what McCraney "was going for" dramatically and emotionally.

One might expect that McCraney would hesitate to hand over a story that foregrounds the protagonist's homosexuality to the straight writer/director Barry Jenkins. But the two men had something else

---

[9] Monica Uszerowicz, "'Moonlight' Story Writer Tarell Alvin McCraney on the Chaos That Is Memory," *Vice*, November 15, 2016, https://www.vice.com/en/article/nz4avz/moonlight-tarell-alvin-mccraney-biographical-story.

[10] Tim Adams, "Moonlight's writer Tarell Alvin McCraney: 'the story needed to be out there.'" *The Guardian*, February 5, 2017, https://www.theguardian.com/film/2017/feb/05/moonlight-writer-tarell-alvin-mccraney-observer-interview.

in common. Jenkins had also grown up in Liberty City, Miami (the setting of the story), and was just a year above McCraney at elementary school, in fact, though the two never met. And this unexpected background shared between McCraney and Jenkins turned out to be more important to the playwright than the sexual orientation of the film's adapter.

There is now frequent discussion about who has the "right" to tell a particular story, especially when that story is someone else's. The truth is that there are no simple answers to that question, as this instance goes to show. The issue is not cut and dried, but rather must be approached case by case, project by project, with a spirit of respectful and creative collaboration at the forefront of the process. In the end, *Moonlight*'s script was substantially reworked by Jenkins, and ultimately McCraney felt that the film expressed all that he wanted to say and more. In fact, at an awards ceremony in Toronto, McCraney had an emotional moment with actor Mahershala Ali, who played Juan. He recalled: "Mahershala was fixing my bow tie backstage . . . and suddenly I started just weeping in his arms. He must have thought I had lost my mind — which I probably had, momentarily. I was back as a six-year-old kid: I think he found a way to bring out something that I had not seen in so long."[11] This is a touching tribute from the original storyteller to the adaptation for the screen — quite an endorsement of the vision and execution of writer/director Barry Jenkins.

It is critical to understand how film adaptations come about. Material may spring from any source, and screenwriters should be open to all avenues of acquisition. And though writers adapting material may not be the original source, it's more than possible to find that personal connection to a story and make the adaptation shine.

---

[11] Adams, "Moonlight's writer."

A Less Traditional Three-Act Structure

The most traditional structure in drama is the three-act structure. Much has been written about the three-act structure, to an extent that I hardly need to add my own explanation. However, a basic understanding of this structure is essential for storytellers[12]:

> The three acts of a book or script represent a beginning, a middle, and an end. In most three-act stories, about 50 percent of the actual storytelling occurs in the second act, with 25 percent of the story falling in the first act and 25 percent falling in the final act.
>
> The first act typically starts with exposition — one or more scenes that establish the world of the story. This act should also establish the ordinary world of the story's main character. Before the act is over, however, an inciting incident should occur — one that pulls the protagonist out of their normal world and into the main action of the story. The act concludes with some sort of turning point that launches the action into act two.

Though the first scene features Juan and other drug dealers on the streets of Liberty City, we almost immediately switch to Little being chased by bullies out for blood. This is Little's ordinary world, where his rescuer Juan is a drug dealer and his hiding place a former crack house — in other words, a hostile environment for a young boy to grow up in.

The inciting incident occurs in a conversation that reveals Little's growing knowledge of the world outside of Juan's house. Initially, Juan and his girlfriend Teresa attempt to protect Little from not only his environment, but also from his unstable and drug addicted mother, Paula, in the hopes of creating a world of love and affection. But when Little asks what "faggot" means and if he is one, the cruelty of the world comes into the caring domestic world offered by Juan.

The final turning point in Act I is when Little follows up his question about "faggots" with one that forces Juan to admits that he

---

[12] The following explanations of the three-act structure are adapted from MasterClass.com: "How to Write Three Act Structure," accessed February 4, 2022, https://www.masterclass.com/articles/how-to-write-three-act-structure.

is not only a drug dealer, but also a drug dealer who supplies Little's mother Paula with drugs. After that painful admission by Juan, Little purposefully leaves Juan's home, the only real home that he has ever known, because his trust in Juan is broken. At that moment, in that scene, Little has to grow up in his rejection of Juan's deception.

> A story's middle act consists of a rising action that leads to a midpoint, then devolves into a crisis. Act two will raise the stakes of the protagonist's journey. The second act typically ends with another turning point that makes it seem as if the protagonist will fail. This is sometimes called the "dark night of the soul."

In act two, we discover that Juan has died and that a now teenaged Little is known as Chiron and is still being bullied relentlessly at his high school. However, Chiron's hope and trust shifts to Kevin, a friend from childhood and currently his only friend in high school. By the story's midpoint, Chiron is fully immersed in his journey, as depicted in the scene between him and Kevin at the beach when their emotional and sexual connection is first made. The "dark night of the soul" in *Moonlight* occurs the very next day in school when Kevin is pressured by bullies into fighting Chiron, whose trust in his newly found lover is broken. The following day builds on this final turning point of act two when Chiron is taken away by police for attacking the head bully, Terrel. At this moment, it seems as if things couldn't get any worse for our protagonist.

> The third act begins with what's known as a pre-climax. This consists of events leading up to a climactic confrontation in which the hero faces a point of no return: They must either prevail or perish. This launches us into the actual climax. Finally, the story deescalates in a denouement, where the events of the climax wind back down into normal life.

Chiron, now a young adult, a drug dealer, is identified as Black and trusts no one. However, when Kevin reaches out to Black, our protagonist decides to reach back and visit his friend, who he has not seen since high school. There, Black admits that he has not been sexually (or emotionally) intimate with anyone since his high school encounter with Kevin. This is the actual climax of the story. The denouement occurs when Black allows Kevin to physically comfort him by gently stroking his head.

While the three-act structure is clear in *Moonlight*, it plays out in the film in a most unusual way. In the first act, the character of Little, played by ten-year-old Alex Hibbert, is introduced. In the second act, a different actor portrays Chiron as he reaches a crisis point in his teenage years. And in the third act, substantially imagined by Jenkins, the adult Chiron has transformed himself into a drug dealer named Black and is depicted by yet another actor. In a review for *The Observer*, Tim Adams wrote: "Physically, the three actors are very different, but Jenkins' concentration on their interior lives means that you don't for a moment feel the disjunction."[13] The first two acts are taken from the original play, but the third and final act is a new creation by Barry Jenkins, a clear departure from the reality of McCraney's life (as he became a writer, not a drug dealer). The foregrounding of the three acts using the different names and ages of one character is a bold choice that could either take an audience out of the story, especially when the third act might be felt as a separate piece, or draw them closer in. And yet, the interiority that Adams so astutely noted ties that final piece together with the others to tell a cohesive tale of a young man's life.

The choice of the three-act structure and casting three different actors in *Moonlight* isn't the first high profile cinematic effort to represent a protagonist with a number of different actors. For example, in the 2007 film *I'm Not There*, six different actors play six different aspects of the music icon Bob Dylan's life and work. Writer/director Todd Haynes took a creative risk that was in some ways overshadowed by its unconventional casting (both male and female actors played the male singer) and at times characterized as a dramatic stunt. By contrast, *Moonlight*'s choice, rather than veering toward the sensational, actually unifies and expands the nature of the story as memory and meditation so that it at once focuses

---

[13] Adams, "Moonlight's writer."

on one character and on a broader shift in representation of young, urban, black males as a group. This approach, this creative choice, helps elevate the film into the realm of high artistic skill.

Unlike how the story is framed in the synopsis, though, the film doesn't begin with a part one intertitle of "Little." It begins instead with the introduction of Juan and his first encounter with Little in a prologue that precedes the naming of part one, particularly interesting because this prologue not only establishes a primary and definitive relationship in Chiron's life, it also introduces the world that Juan and Little exist in — one of drugs and violence, but also of caring and nurturing. Viewers might expect that all these qualities could not coexist in such a relatively short sequence, but they do — and very memorably, as the time between Little and Juan lasts only from the prologue through the first act but reverberates throughout the entire film. It should also be noted that the jumps in narrative at the two subsequent act breaks are consistent with the first, the older version of the character appearing before the character is "announced" with the intertitle of the name and part number. In this way, the transitions move more smoothly, with a bridge of sorts that prevents the act breaks from being too abrupt or potentially becoming confusing.

Kevin appears in all three parts, as rescuer, friend, confidant, and lover. Paula appears in all three segments as well, with mixed characteristics. Basically, Paula's relationship with Chiron is a subplot (very important, but still a subplot), while Chiron's relationship with Kevin makes up the main plot. And I would argue that Chiron's relationship with Juan is the most important subplot, even though Juan is physically absent from the last two acts. Juan's impact on Chiron's life is profound, as is clear in Part III when Chiron has made himself over physically to look like Juan in the same role of drug dealer.

Part one's introduction of Chiron, in which he explains that he's called Little, is very significant in that we begin to understand this is a world where identities are determined by others. The ordinary world of the protagonist must be established right away in a script, first with character descriptions that are evocative but not too specific so as to limit casting choices. For example, Juan is described as "30s, some sort of Afro-Latino thing about him," Little as a "similarly aged [to those chasing him] (adolescent, 12/13 years old) but smaller, a runt." At least in these two instances, the most distinctive physical characteristics that the actors need to have — the things that others would notice about them — are clearly stated.

The prologue further sets up the world of street drug dealers and the danger lurking beneath the surface as Juan's domain. He's the confident leader, but of a terrible enterprise. He initially comes across as callous and heartless, especially to his underlings and addicts, in a potentially stereotypical scene that audiences have seen time and time again in the urban landscape. However, the film switches to an adjacent scene, equally fraught with danger, that takes its form in an all-out chase, with Little as the unfortunate target of a group of toughs. The script description distinguishes this instance of bullying as "not a game, more like a hunt." Most cinematic chases are saved for the second or sometimes third act, but we are still in the prologue, the setup. Immediately, we are invested in this story and shown the palpable terror of our young protagonist, as well as the subsequent reassuring kindness of Juan that coaxes Little out of the abandoned crack house where he finds temporary refuge. This first meeting between Little and Juan begins the tender process that allows the boy to begin to show trust and love.

There are a number of questions that need to be answered in part two, in which Chiron is shown not in his ordinary world as Little but fully immersed in the world of high school adolescence after moving on from his childhood rescuer. And the answers to these questions reveal Chiron's vulnerability, his pain, and a loneliness typical of a teenager who lacks any friends his own age. Will Chiron return to Juan? Yes and no. He returns to Juan's house, but Juan has died. Will Chiron overcome the bullying at school, and more specifically a bully named Terrel? Not really; he strikes out, but must pay the price of incarceration as a juvenile delinquent. Will

Chiron's situation at home with his mother Paula get better? Not in this act; his situation stays the same as in part one. Will Chiron find at least one friend at school? Yes, and more, but it doesn't last. Chiron is intimate with Kevin but is also betrayed by him when Kevin is pressured by bullies to beat Chiron up in a violent "game."

Even though we begin the second act with several questions, and even though they are all answered to some extent, the overarching and most urgent question is whether Chiron will find someone to love and trust. The main plot of this act concerns only the friendship, attraction, intimacy, and betrayal between Chiron and Kevin. Traditionally, act two introduces a romantic subplot for the protagonist. However, Chiron's same-sex romantic longing for Kevin is not merely a subplot, it exists at the center of his maturation and sense of well-being. The rising action in part two introduces Kevin as a love object, someone Chiron has known since he was Little, and now someone who is described in the screenplay as being a "smooth-as-hell-looking teen." The midpoint dramatizes both the emotional and physical intimacy between the teen boys. It is a rare moment of safety and tenderness that is effectively framed between the numerous attacks, taunts, and intimidation by the school bullies. We end the act with Chiron striking out, fighting back against his main tormentor Terrel, but the win is momentary when he pays the heavy price of juvenile incarceration. Chiron doesn't win in love or war. But we empathize with his attempts to assert his needs and strength.

Part three begins with a resolution of a subplot even more important in the screenplay than in the finished film: the relationship between Chiron (now called Black) and his mother, and his forgiveness of her. He visits her in rehab, and she tells him that she is sorry for the way she treated him, that she loves him, but that he doesn't have to love her back after all that she's done. But most importantly, Paula addresses the issue of trust with Black in a way that allows the subplot to reflect back on the questions of the main plot: "I am your mother, ain't I? You can talk to me if you want to? Or at least somebody, you got to trust somebody, you hear?" This is still the central question for our protagonist: Will he find someone that he can love and trust?

Another subplot comes full circle through Black, who has become exactly what he walked away from with Juan: a drug dealer. But the difference could be Kevin, and the fact that Black drives from his new home in Atlanta, Georgia, back to Florida to see him. Kevin does not approve of Black's pushing drugs and reveals that he's been married and has a child. The conversation between them is a bit awkward, but the subtext is of two men who have a great deal of love and affection for one another. A key moment of the story is when Black admits that he has never been intimate with anyone since Kevin. This both shows that Black hasn't let himself care for anyone since Kevin and that he has continued caring for Kevin over the years. The climax addresses the question of whether Black, in the new version of himself, can even be reached emotionally, whether he can love and trust again. This is where the screenplay and film significantly diverge. As laid out in the script, Kevin and Black make love in the dark, the audience only able to hear them. In the finished film, Kevin takes Black and gently strokes his head. Each ending is somewhat open, but both the script and film versions answer that yes: Black's emotional and physical vulnerability is reawakened in this meeting with Kevin.

In many ways, the film version speaks more to Black's entire journey, as Little, Chiron, and Black, as Kevin's gesture almost evokes a sense of giving comfort to a child. And so the resolution or denouement that rests in the lyrical final image of Little at the edge of the ocean makes complete sense. It harkens back to the time when Black as Little from the opening act was fully open and capable of trusting and loving, especially in the moonlight.

Naming and Identity

One of the more distinctive elements of Moonlight is the act of naming — or perhaps a better way to put it is the act of *being named* — as both a structural element and character trait. Chiron's self-introduction is telling in the way that it's worded:

> LITTLE: My name Chiron. (and) But people call me Little.
>
> TERESA: I'm gon' call you by your name.
>
> Little shrugs.

The disconnect for Chiron between his given name and what the people in his world call him is clear, his identity lying somewhere in between, somewhere unknown. And the shrug that is indicated in the script is proof that he has given up, at least momentarily, on asserting himself even on something as basic as his name.

In a subsequent scene with Juan, Little comments that he recognizes Juan's name as Spanish but is confused by his father figure's African American appearance:

> LITTLE: Okay . . . why your name Juan?
>
> JUAN: How you mean?
>
> LITTLE: Juan is like a Spanish name. (and after a thought) But you black just like me.

This amuses Juan, who then uses this moment to teach Little about the fact that "it's black people everywhere, you remember that, okay?" and also explains that he himself is from Cuba. But that scene also goes even further into the act of being named by others. This time, a nickname comes from an old lady Juan knew when he was a little boy in Cuba. Juan recalls: "Then she smiled and she say, 'Running around catching up all this light. In moonlight,' she say, 'black boys look blue. You blue,' she say. 'That's what I'm gone call you: Blue.'" Juan and Little's conversation about Juan's given name inspires Juan to become a benevolent teacher about his race and share the story about his nickname, Blue, from a personal childhood memory, indicating a growing vulnerability and strong identification with Little. In other words, the act of being named in these instances reveals character as well as the nature of relationships.

In fact, one of the most powerful and memorable scenes that involves naming comes at the end of part one through a major plot point, a loss of innocence that moves Little into the next phase of his young life:

LITTLE: What's a faggot?

JUAN: A faggot is . . . a word used to make gay people feel bad.

LITTLE: Am I a faggot?

JUAN: No. You're not a faggot. (and) You can be gay, but . . . you don't have to let nobody call you a faggot.

It is important to note here that Jenkins' prior characterization of Juan as both black and Cuban as well as Little as black and gay effectively introduce the concept of intersectionality. People rarely identify with only one characteristic, but rather as a combination of personal traits and qualities. The most successful characterizations in film often offer depictions where multiple identities intersect in unexpected ways (such as the Asian female martial artists in *Crouching Tiger Hidden Dragon* (2000), in addition to other qualities that make them more complex and multidimensional). And in rejecting the name "faggot" on Little's behalf, acknowledging Little's multiple identities, Juan gives voice to an expression of love between the two.

However, this leads to another question about Juan being a drug dealer (an additional aspect of his identity) and Little's mom being on drugs. Little puts these two things together as if for the first time and leaves his surrogate parent's home with the painful truth in another major turning point. He is growing up and away from Juan. The next time we see Little, he is no longer Little but Chiron the teenager, and Juan is dead.

When Chiron returns to Juan's house at the beginning of part two, he and Teresa spar about his name. Initially, she calls him Chiron. Yet in conversation she refers to him as Little, almost as if nostalgic for their shared past with Juan, to which he responds,

"Don't call me that." Teresa jokes that he's "grown now" so the name doesn't fit anymore, but that he has to earn the right to be something different with a new name. She says, "You gotta make your name true, understand?" This scene functions as a bridge between the first two acts of the story, helping the viewers shift their focus from Little and Juan to Chiron and Kevin. In fact, the last scene before the part two intertitle introducing Chiron shows Kevin becoming a more dominant character, as indicated by introducing another name for Chiron, affectionately calling him "Black" when he says goodbye at school.

Nicknames work to great dramatic effect to reveal how characters feel about themselves or identify, as well as how characters feel about one another. Because Chiron says Little is what "they" call him when we first hear that name, it's clear how Chiron feels about that name. "They" refers to everyone in the community who doesn't see him for who he is. Similarly, Juan shares how he got the nickname Blue through a story about his childhood in Cuba when he was just a boy like Little. The nickname reveals the title of the play on which the movie was based, as mentioned, but more than this, Juan is sharing that he, too, was named by others. And sometimes, Juan calls Little "lil' man," as when teaching him how to swim, for encouragement and strength.

But Kevin's nickname for Chiron, "Black," confuses him. Chiron even asks at one point why Kevin keeps calling him that. Kevin explains simply that it's his nickname for Chiron, not really explaining at all. "You don't like it?" he asks. Chiron responds with a simple shrug. It seems like another instance of being named by someone else, but it is qualitatively different because Kevin cares whether Chiron likes it or not. In this way, Kevin seems to be offering a nickname rather than imposing an identity, like the community did with Little. Ultimately, as noted in the script, Chiron accepts the name Kevin gave him and even has a vanity license plate with the name "Black." This license plate is also an indication that even though he would at first glance appear to have moved on in the third act, he is still very much attached to Kevin and appreciates that Kevin gave him a name and an identity that suits him.

Upending Urban Stereotypes

The setting of *Moonlight* is very unique, particularly in the context of other urban African American male coming-of-age film representations. *Moonlight* does contain elements of the archetypal urban landscape, with its inclusion of pervasive poverty, neglect, criminal activity, and drug use. And yet, the specificity of Liberty City, a low-rise housing project in north Miami, contributes to the unusual elements, such as brightly painted homes that capture the feel of the 1980s. In fact, Barry Jenkins, after being questioned about recreating the economically depressed look of the projects at that time, states how this wasn't difficult at all because "it still looks exactly the same now."[14] Usually the idea of the city of Miami conjures up images of glamorous beaches with much wealth and generally opulent surroundings, which stands in stark contrast to the poverty-stricken housing project in Liberty City depicted here, a location that both Tarell McCraney and Barry Jenkins know very well. Tarell McCraney in an interview from *Deadline* reflects:

> Barry's only nine months older than me so we're in the same schools at the same time. We were certainly under the same moon, so the same moon that I was talking to as a kid was shining on him playing football in the same lot that I was running away from bullies. A lot of other mothers were suffering from addiction pretty much at the same time that we were both living in the same projects three blocks away.[15]

McCraney's mention of talking to the moon as a kid when he describes his life in Liberty City perhaps was an indication of things to come with this project, where key moments in the narrative and, of course, the title refer back to the transformative power of moonlight. Jenkins uses an exceptional combination of elements (both

---

[14] Adams, "Moonlight's writer."

[15] Amanda N'Duka, "Tarell Alvin McCraney on 'Moonlight's' Message: "I Think People Were Hungry for That," *Deadline*, February 17, 2017, https://deadline.com/2017/02/tarell-alvin-mccraney-moonlight-barry-jenkins-a24-oscars-interview-1201915105.

emotional and material) taken from an impoverished community; the natural beauty of the moonlight and the ocean in particular is accessible to all, regardless of income level or social status. The characters in *Moonlight* are drawn to the "endless stretch" of the ocean. It's where Juan gently teaches Little how to swim (and trust) by having him float on top of the water as he holds and guides him. After Juan and Little sit on the shore and talk, the description notes "the moon making its first appearance on the horizon — sound of the waves running back and forth, to and from shore."

The vivid description of the setting in the screenplay suggests the overwhelming splendor of nature in the face of so much hardship for these characters. In this way, *Moonlight* breaks with the stereotypical cinematic depiction of a relentlessly claustrophobic urban setting made of concrete, where any element of nature is suppressed or withheld. So, too, does the scene of intimacy between Kevin and Chiron break the typical depiction of urban African American males. The natural beauty of the moonlight, ocean, and beach all conspire to create a most romantic setting for the couple. The very distinctive setting adds a welcome dimension and respite from the more familiar elements of the drug-filled neighborhood that allow Chiron no rest, no joy.

Symbolism

Symbolism is used to great effect in *Moonlight* to establish or reinforce character traits, reveal relationships, and provide powerful metaphors at key points in the plot. Some incorrectly think symbolism is just a literary device, not to be used in screenplays, but *Moonlight* makes it clear this is not the case. Films can be filled with symbolism that seeks to immerse the audience more deeply into the narrative. For example, the element of food appears at particular dramatic moments in the film to tell us more about what characters are needing and giving. In the scene with Juan and Little at the first restaurant they visit together, a local diner, Juan tries to find out more about this young stranger who he rescued — his name and where he lives, to begin with — as he voraciously eats his meal. The description reflects the depths of Little's hunger:

```
Little just eating, not a single care in
the world but this meal.

JUAN: You not gon' tell me what you' name
is?

Nothing. Little finishing a drumstick,
dips a biscuit into the gravy there. He's
hungry.
```

Unsuccessful, Juan finally pulls Little's tray of food away from him to try and get him to talk, but he immediately apologizes when he sees Little reaction "just looking down at the empty table before him." Juan suddenly understands the depth of his hunger and the neglect of a child's basic needs. His dramatic response is about much more than food. It's indicative of Little's past and present state of mind and body.

Not coincidentally, Kevin has become a cook in Part III, a master of what Black hungers for in more ways than one. When he offers to fix him a meal, "a chef's special," he is offering much more than food; he is offering a gift of affection and love. Just as with Juan and Teresa, Black accepts and cleans his plate. By now we know his hunger is both internal and external, extending to both body and heart. How appropriate that the scene right after we first meet Little running away, he is eating ravenously. And so, with the final scene he consumes a meal made especially just for him. In both cases, he is cared for and nurtured through food.

Water is also a crucial element and symbol of rebirth, self-care, and communion. The swimming scene with Juan in the ocean could be said to be a rebirth of Little. Juan guides Little almost as if he were an infant, with great gentleness and care. The image of Juan holding Little in the water has become iconic and representative of the closeness and trust in the relationship between these two characters. This moment is recalled in the final image of the film of young Little going into the ocean alone, though not before we see his gaze of openness and trust, a gift from Juan. The final moment is described in the screenplay thusly:

```
Little turning from us, his form and
movement slowly, steadily melding into the
flow of light and waves as he heads out
into the ocean and we . . . FADE TO BLACK.
```

The ocean in this moment is love, which Little first learned to experience at that time in his life, and because this image comes after his encounter with the adult Kevin, we see how the later experience reflects that love, signaling both depth and endless possibilities.

Earlier in the film, Little gives himself a bath using dishwashing liquid. The scene is an extended one, showing how Little methodically gets hot water from a five-gallon pot on the stove and then pours it into a bathtub that's already about a quarter filled with water. His movements are sure and solitary. We can tell that he has had to do this many times, taking care of himself when his mother is unavailable because of drugs. This scene underscores Little's peaceful feeling in the water and yet contrasts the scene with Juan because here Little seems so alone.

Finally, the water provides both the subject leading up to and the backdrop for Kevin and Chiron's sexual encounter. They talk about how good the ocean breeze feels, how they can sometimes feel it in the hood, how everybody there just wants to feel it. The sound of the ocean is indicated in the screenplay as important for the seductive nature of the scene. It calls for the "sound of the ocean, sound of the wind running through the reeds, the night." The waves moving in and out also provide an externalized emotional push and pull for their first intimate encounter. It is the dominant element of this memorable scene in which the two are overtaken by their own emotional and physical natures as well as by the surrounding sensations of this natural environment.

There is so much at work in this film that comes together to make the origin story profoundly deeper and richer through the inventive use of story structure (particularly the choice of a fore-grounded three-act structure), unusual settings (for an urban drama), and impactful symbolism. These elements produce a story that needs to be told, that adds to our understanding of humanity in an innovative and untraditional way. It's diverse not only in the choice of subject matter of an underrepresented group and the layering of diverse identities but also in the creative ways that the story was realized. And we are all the better for witnessing the end product.

CHAPTER TWO

The Haunted Legacy of Slavery

in *GET OUT* (2017)

*"I had set out to write something fun that did something
mischievous, but then I realized, 'Oh fuck, if this ever actually gets
made, it's going to be so important.'"*

— Jordan Peele

The preceding quote from Academy Award–winning screenwriter Jordan Peele reflects his incredulous attitude when realizing the potential significance that *Get Out*, a film that uniquely blends the genre of horror with racial satire, might possess.

Jordan Peele was raised in Manhattan and from an early age was interested in performing and movies. After graduating high school in 1997, he enrolled at Sarah Lawrence College but soon left school after he took a class on comedy to pursue a career in comedy full time. Peele later became a member of an improv group, Boom Chicago (based in Amsterdam). In 2002 during a "Comedy Swap" between Boom Chicago and Second City theater in Chicago, Peele met Keegan-Michael Key, and the next year they both performed on the sketch comedy show *MADtv*. While Peele remained on the show until 2008, he eventually reteamed with Key to create the Comedy Central series *Key and Peele* from 2012 to 2015. The show won a number of awards, such as a Peabody Award and an Emmy Award. Peele also starred with Key in the comedy film *Keanu*, which Peele also co-wrote.[1]

Peele's debut as a director was with the horror movie *Get Out*. The premise involves a young black man who visits his white girlfriend's family, only to find they plan to replace his brain with a white person's.[2] His initial inspiration went back to the 2008 primary fight between Barak Obama and Hillary Clinton. He says that he was looking at gender and race as two parallel civil rights movements, racism and sexism as two parallel problems, so he thought that if others could make movies "as entertaining as *Rosemary's Baby* and *The Stepford Wives*, which have what should be an equally offensive notion — that men are going to conspire again women — you could do it with race."[3] Peele got a script draft done in two months. He says that there were many years of just conceiving the movie so that by the time he sat down to write, he knew every scene. Then, after getting halfway through the draft, he decided that he had to also direct the film, thinking, "I have seen so few horror movies where a black person has been given the director's chair that I realized, *Why not me? I know this thing.*"[4]

According to Jason Blum, reporting in *Vulture*, "*Get Out* was shot in just 23 days on a budget of $4.5 million." But it was the second-highest grossing horror movie of 2017, making $255 million at the box office. "Anyone who loves scary movies went to see *Get*

---

[1] Patricia Bauer, "Jordan Peele," *Encyclopedia Britannica*, accessed October 31, 2021, https://www.britannica.com/biography/Jordan-Peele.
[2] Bauer, "Jordan Peele."
[3] Jada Yuan and Hunter Harris, "The First Great Movie of the Trump Era," *Vulture*, accessed February 4, 2022, https://www.vulture.com/article/get-out-oral-history-jordan-peele.html.
[4] Yuan and Hunter, "The First Great Movie."

Out, but then a whole bigger, broader audience also went. That's the only way you see that kind of growth," he wrote.[5]

An excellent resource on this film is *Get Out: The Complete Annotated Screenplay* by Jordan Peele, which contains the entire script with notes by Peele, who wrote and directed the film, as well as a number of significant points regarding his creative process. One of the most striking elements of Peele's creative process detailed in the book includes his stated cinematic influences, films ranging from *Guess Who's Coming to Dinner* (1967) to *Rosemary's Baby* (1968) to *The Stepford Wives* (1975). These older films piqued Peele's interest because they "all had this classic storytelling feel that I wanted to emulate and modernize."[6]

According to Peele, *Get Out* took almost ten years to complete, with a number of important creative breakthroughs along the way. Peele explains how he worked on the script off and on, taking breaks from writing for months at times, understanding the setup but not necessarily where the story was headed, only gradually over time adding new elements. Peele confesses that "there was no real engine behind it — it was just something I was working on and that was teaching me to be a better writer."[7]

Peele's own candid comments about his motivations, limitations, and, most importantly, persistence emphasize that there is no "one size fits all" process of screenwriting or great storytelling. The only commonality, I believe, is sustained effort and (even with an original screenplay) research, if only to discover or rediscover similar films that could become influential to your individual approach to your story, as Peele found with *Rosemary's Baby* and *The Stepford Wives*. Finally, Peele discovered that he needed a specific name for the type of genre *Get Out* offers to movie audiences: "I was trying to figure out what genre this movie was, and horror didn't quite do it. Psychological thriller didn't do it, and so I thought, *Social thriller*. The bad guy is society — these things that are innate in all of us, and

---

[5] Yuan and Hunter, "The First Great Movie."
[6] Jordan Peele, *Get Out: The Complete Annotated Screenplay* (Inventory Press, 2019).
[7] Peele, *Get Out: The Complete Annotated Screenplay*.

provide good things, but ultimately prove that humans are always going to be barbaric, to an extent. I think I coined the term social thriller, but I definitely didn't invent it."[8] The following synopsis of *Get Out* reveals a story that creates a world of its own, a world commenting on both past racial trauma as well as a contemporary reality that attempts to conceal the racism of the present.

SYNOPSIS

In the opening scene a young black man named Andre is walking alone at night through a quiet suburban street. A little sports car pulls up and starts slowly tracking him. From out of nowhere, a man in a medieval helmet attacks Andre, who immediately becomes unconscious and drags his body to the car.

A young African American man, Chris, prepares to go with his white girlfriend, Rose, to visit her family for the weekend. When he finds out that she has not told her family that he is black, he is wary, but she reassures him that they are incredibly liberal and "would have voted for Obama for a third time." On the drive there, the car hits a deer and the police investigate Chris rather than Rose, who was actually driving. Rose protests and the police leave, and Chris comments that he enjoyed how Rose "took charge" in that situation.

Finally, they get to Rose's parents' estate, and her parents, Dean and Missy Armitage, are surprised but very accepting of Chris. But when Chris and Dean take a walk around the grounds of the estate, it is very noticeable that the house staff are black, from the groundskeeper Walter to the maid Georgina. Dean is slightly embarrassed because "it looks bad," and Chris thinks it is a little weird but accepts the situation. Chris tries to connect with both the

---

[8] Yuan and Hunter, "The First Great Movie."

groundskeeper and the maid, who come across very stiff and robotic, acting strange and distant.

After dinner that night, Rose's brother Jeremy attends but is drunk and gets aggressive toward Chris, to the discomfort of Dean, Missy, and Rose, who nevertheless do nothing to stop him. That night, Chris takes a walk around the grounds and sees Walter the groundskeeper running toward him, then suddenly running in another direction. Spooked and feeling a bit weird, Chris goes back into the house but runs into Rose's mother Missy, a therapist who hypnotizes him against his will. It's a very scary experience for Chris, who goes into "the sunken place," a black hole where he can only see life from a distance.

The next morning, Chris wakes in a cold sweat and tries to tell Rose what happened to him the previous night. She says she doesn't understand what he's talking about, so he gives up trying to explain it to her. Later, an annual garden party has been planned, though Rose is surprised and not at all happy about it. At the party, Chris is the main attraction simply because he's African American. He is repeatedly asked what he thinks as an African American man on different issues, from sexual prowess to general questions about what it's like to be black. Most of the people at the party are middle-aged and older, which strikes Chris as very strange. Finally, Chris sees another black male guest at the party and tries to connect with him. However, the man (who looks like Andre, the character from the beginning of the film, but is now called Logan) is noticeably stiff and uses old-fashioned language to express his thoughts. Despite Chris' best efforts, Andre treats him like he would any of the white guests. After a Japanese guest asks Chris "whether there are more advantages or disadvantages in being black," a very irritated Chris poses the questions to Andre, who struggles to answer the question and seems very confused by it. He then appears disturbed, with blood running out of one nostril, and urgently begs Chris to "get out, get the fuck out of here while you still can." The white guests with Andre quickly take him away from Chris, who is very alarmed and unnerved at his sudden outburst. The party guests wait inside the house for Andre to reemerge. When he does, he is apologetic, claiming that he had a seizure, nothing more. Chris doesn't believe this, though he pretends to in front of the other guests.

When Chris and Rose are alone, Chris states for the first time that he wants to leave. Rose reluctantly agrees. Back at the house, Dean is holding a silent auction with his guests. Next to him is a picture of Chris. When packing to leave, Chris discovers old photos of Rose with a number of other black men, including Walter, and Georgina. The two look completely different. Chris now knows that Rose has been lying to him about him being her first black boyfriend.

When Chris and Rose confront her family, who strongly object to them leaving, Rose suddenly can't find her car keys. Then she stops looking and calmly says, "You know I can't give you the keys." At this point, Chris know for sure that Rose is in on whatever is going on at the house. Rose's brother Jeremy roughly grabs Chris, taking him down to the basement. Waking up, Chris finds himself tied to a chair in a game room in front of a vintage TV set. On the screen an old man, Rose's grandfather, talks of a procedure, a brain transplant into a black host body, that gives eternal life. Chris is horrified until he hears the "ting" of a spoon hitting a teacup, as when Missy first hypnotized him, that renders him unconscious. Again and again Chris struggles with the bonds around his wrists and feet, but as soon as he begins to make any sort of progress, the sound of the spoon hitting the teacup knocks him out.

One of the guests, Jim, who Chris had spoken to at the party, explains that he will be the recipient of Chris' brain and eyes because his own are failing, and also because Chris has a great photographer's eye. Finally, we see Chris has been scratching and removing the stuffing from the chair he is tied to and putting it in his ears so that he doesn't hear the sound that makes him unconscious. When Rose's brother Jeremy comes to get Chris for the brain swap surgery, Chris pretends to be unconscious but then suddenly attacks Jeremy, breaking free of the room.

Dean Armitage is prepping Jim for the surgery as Chris tries to get out of the house. He fights off and kills Jeremy, as well as Dean and Missy Armitage and finally Rose, who he hesitates a bit to kill. However, Walter steps in to kill her and then shoot himself, saving Chris' life. A police car suddenly pulls up, but it turns out to be Rod, Chris' friend from the city, who has come to take him back home. Rod tells Chris that he knew something was suspicious. They drive off and away from the estate.

Conventions of Horror

In order to unpack the brilliance of the film *Get Out*, we must first understand the basic workings of the horror genre. Story Grid editor Rachelle Ramirez in her article "Secrets of the Horror Genre" outlines the genre using *Get Out*. According to Ramirez, the structure of a successful horror script must follow a number of specific rules:

- **"Begin in a world where the protagonist is shown doing something normal."** In *Get Out*, our protagonist, African American photographer Chris, is preparing to leave with his white girlfriend Rose for the weekend to meet her parents.
- **"Demonstrate a fear or flaw to establish empathy. We need to want them to live."** Chris is shown as both tense and vulnerable (though not exactly fearful) through his interaction with the police on the way to Rose's parents' house.

- **"Demonstrate the character's want clearly."** Chris wants to be accepted by Rose's family, and even more wants to connect with the other black people on the estate (either working or visiting guests) to help control his racial anxiety and isolation.
- **"Create a setting that isolates the protagonist. Inability to obtain outside help is key."** The Armitage estate is explicitly described as isolated, with only Chris' friend Rod from New York City occasionally available by his cell phone.
- **"Introduce supporting characters that are interesting and multidimensional."** All supporting characters in *Get Out* are interesting, including Rose's parents (Dean, a conflicted liberal, and Missy, a therapist specializing in hypnosis); Georgina, the maid, and Walter, the groundskeeper, both strangely odd in completely different ways; Andre/Logan, from his first brief appearance at the beginning of the film to his dramatic shift at the Armitage garden party; and Rod, Chris' best friend, who lends some much needed humor even while only appearing a few times throughout the narrative.
- **"Foreshadow the dangers to come by teasing the audience. Make them jump at scenes that appear scary but turn out to be relatively harmless."** Two instances where things appear to be threatening but wind up not to be so are during Chris' first night at the estate while taking a walk when he sees Walter running toward him, only to have the groundskeeper suddenly turn away in another direction, and when Georgina seems to see Chris and Walter but is actually looking at her own reflection.
- **"The inciting incident that begins the protagonist's acceptance of 'adventure' in this genre comes in the guise of a warning . . . by ignoring the warning, the protagonist inadvertently accepts their leading role in the story."** Missy hypnotizing Chris after his walk the first night, especially sending him to that sunken place, is a major warning that Chris shrugs off the next morning.
- **"In Act II, you will slowly expose your protagonist to greater and greater danger due to the bad choices they make."** Simply

staying at the estate puts Chris in more and more danger as he mingles with strangely predatory party guests and finds his cell phone unplugged with a dead battery, leading up to the silent auction where he is the object of the bidding.

- **"The monster or evil forces keep attacking until the protagonist's situation appears hopeless in the All-Is-Lost scene at the midpoint of Act II."** This occurs when Chris is tied to a chair, unable to escape from the television in front of him describing the brain swap that he is to be prepared for. All of this is due to Missy's hypnotic power over Chris from the first night, throwing him into unconsciousness repeatedly and rendering him helpless.

- **"There is a false ending. Your protagonist may mistakenly think that another more capable character will solve it for them only to discover that it's still up to the protagonist."** This happens when Walter shoots Rose and then himself, leaving Chris to fend for himself.

- **"Your climax will include how the protagonist fights the monster/evil forces usually by outsmarting these figures. They rise to the challenge through confronting their fear or flaw and survive or fail to rise to the challenge and die."** Rose turns out to be still alive. Chris strangles her in self-defense almost to the point of death and leaves her to die.

- **"At the end, you leave your audience with information that evil is never entirely defeated. You could be next."** Chris' friend, Rod, shows up in a police car from New York to rescue Chris from the carnage while stating that he should have never gone to the Armitage estate in the first place.[9]

These elements of the horror genre just scratch the surface of how creative and innovative the genre can be, not even touching on the possibilities offered with the injection of satire or social commentary. And *Get Out* has the latter in abundance, as well as wickedly

---

[9] Rachelle Ramirez, "Secrets of the Horror Genre," Story Grid, accessed February 4, 2022, https://storygrid.com/secrets-of-the-horror-genre/.

dark humor. The forces of evil in *Get Out* are presented as rational and explainable, unlike other horror vehicles that feature the supernatural, spiritual, and monstrous, or even entire "slasher" franchises where gratuitous violence reigns for no apparent reason. The horror in *Get Out*, in being more real and specifically in utilizing the situational conflicts and circumstances of a distinctly interracial society, lingers in the imagination long after viewing.

Four-Act Structure

Jordan Peele's screenplay for *Get Out* is written in four acts, as opposed to the more common three-act structure. In reality, the three-act structure is often presented in four parts, in particular by Syd Field in his books on screenwriting. Field terms these four parts Act I, Act IIa, Act IIb, and Act III.[10] In *Get Out*, Act I is relatively short, including what I like to call the prologue when Andre gets kidnapped while lost in the suburbs at night, then the ride to the Armitage house with the deer's death and encounter with police along the way. Act II, Field's IIa, is signaled by Chris and Rose's arrival at the Armitage home. Act III (IIb), the longest Act in the screenplay, begins with Chris' first encounter with Andre/Logan at the party and ends with Chris strapped to the chair in front of a TV screen while Rod attempts to find out what's happened to Chris during a strange and aborted phone conversation with Rose. Act IV (or III) begins with Jim Hudson on the TV screen explaining their planned brain-swapping surgical procedure to Chris.

What the four-part structure allows for in *Get Out* is a more extended "crisis" for the protagonist in Act III (after the setup in Act I and rising action of Act II) before a shorter climax and resolution in Act IV. This extended crisis addresses both external and internal conflicts at play in Chris' character development. The "get out!" that Andre/Logan screams at Chris starts the ball rolling, as Chris begins to face an externalized, physical threat. He wants to leave the Armitage house soon after his final encounter with Andre/Logan but is not

---

[10] Syd Field, *Screenplay: The Foundations of Screenwriting* (Delta: 2005).

allowed to; further, he becomes the subject of Missy's hypnotic mind control and is strapped in a chair, forced to watch a television screen that details the Armitage family's diabolical plans. Both these elements — external (Chris' physical entrapment) and internal (Chris' mind going in and out of consciousness) — are neatly brought together in this extended sequence. Missy's manipulation of Chris' emotional mind is shown to be a very powerful evil force that he must overcome in order to become whole and, most urgently, now to save his own life. In addition, the extended Act III provides space for Rod's role to be factored in as he tries, in vain, to convince others what he knows in his gut to be true, that his friend is in mortal danger. Suspense is allowed to build to a fever pitch as the audience wonders if Chris will be able to escape the fate of Georgina, Walter, and Andre/Logan in a situation that appears completely hopeless. As the horror genre structural conventions dictate, Rod's encounter with the police is set up almost as a false ending that makes us think he might be able to solve Chris' predicament, only for Rod to discover that it's still up to Chris to save himself.

All of this detail prepares us so well for the climax, when "the protagonist fights the evil forces . . . They rise to the challenge through confronting their fear or flaw and survive or fail to rise to the challenge and die."[11] Notably, in *The Stepford Wives*, Joanna ultimately fails to rise to the challenge and "dies," only to become yet another Stepford Wife. But that type of resolution does not occur in the final version of *Get Out*; Chris makes it out. In an alternate ending, he survived the Armitages' attempt to steal his soul but was taken to jail. That ending did not test well, according to Jordan Peele, which is why he changed it to feature Rod's humorous line: "Man, I told you not to go in that house."[12]

---

[11] Ramirez, "Secrets of the Horror Genre."
[12] Peele, *Get Out: The Complete Annotated Screenplay*.

Premise and Setup

The entire premise of the story hinges on the societal "problem" of whether the African American Chris will be accepted by his white girlfriend's family. It plays upon the subgenre of "meet the parents" comedy movies that includes *Meet the Parents* (2000), *Meet the Fockers* (2004), *Guess Who* (2005), *Little Fockers* (2010), and *The Big Wedding* (2013). *Guess Who* is an interesting case because it harkens back to the film *Guess Who's Coming to Dinner* (even taking its title from the first two words of the 1960s film) but reverses the racial dynamics, with Ashton Kutcher hoping to impress his fiancée's father, played by Bernie Mac.

Chris' race is the first and most prominent element that sets into motion the plot of the film. We see the first instance of societal conflict in the form of Chris' encounter with the police on the road to the estate, occurring before he has a chance to meet Rose's family — the conflict pervades the film even apart from his goal to "meet the parents." In this scene, Rose takes charge and challenges the racism of the police officer, who backs off from asking for Chris' driver's license when he wasn't driving the car.

After arriving at the home of Rose's parents, Chris seeks to gain their acceptance. Let's be clear, Rose's parents are depicted initially as left-of-center liberals. They appear in no way overtly racist in the traditional sense. This choice highlights the danger in the assumption that all liberals are natural allies for African Americans. Rose's parents remain another key societal hurdle that Chris has to overcome because of his race. At the garden party the next day, Chris is polite, though somewhat repelled by the many older white guests who seem to feel that being black is "in fashion" or something exotic. The one exception is a Japanese man at the party who asks an exasperated Chris (at this point weary of answering questions about his race) whether he thinks "being black has more advantages or disadvantages" — a question which Chris punts to a somewhat bewildered Andre/Logan. It is striking that an Asian man is thrown into the racial mix at the Armitage party (as well as the auction occurring later), complicating the black-white binary. This inclusion is in part an homage to the final scene in *Rosemary's Baby*, in which a Japanese man (portrayed with a camera, like a tourist) joins with the other Satanic worshippers at a gathering to welcome the baby. In that film, his presence seems to cue an international dimension, as if the worshippers are from all over the world, whereas in *Get Out*, there seems to be an attempt to subtly extend the Armitages' way of thinking to other non-black people.

Chris' character is set up as internally vulnerable in ways that we don't fully grasp at first as an audience. The first indication occurs in one of his first conversations with Rose's parents, particularly her mother, Missy.

```
DEAN (to Chris): And what do your parents
do?

CHRIS: My dad was never really in the
picture. My mom passed away when I was
11 . . . Hit-and-run.

MISSY: How did she die?

CHRIS: Hit-and-Run.

DEAN: So young, too.

CHRIS: — Actually I don't remember a whole
lot from that time.

MISSY: It's okay. We don't need to talk
about that.

Missy stirs her glass. The spoon hits the
side of the glass creating a small . . .

Ting ting. Ting ting.

Chris and Missy share a comforting look.
They have an unspoken connection.
```

The parental story that Chris relays introduces his character's tragic backstory and reinforces his aloneness in the world; he is an orphan, and from a young age. This makes him especially vulnerable to another intact family, even if not of his own race. And, significantly, we are also introduced to Missy's hypnotic cue — her spoon hitting the side of a glass or tea cup. This exchange does a couple of things in a very short amount of time. It introduces an internal vulnerability and struggle for our main character Chris to overcome, the internal development that he must undergo over the course of the film, while subtly introducing the mode of his emotional undoing, the simple gesture of Missy's spoon softly hitting her glass. Through this backstory, Missy will hypnotize and control Chris until he takes control and is able to save himself.

The trauma of Chris' mother's death is repeated in the scene near the end the film in which Chris literally runs over Georgina — "who, in the night, seemed to come out of nowhere," as the screenplay says — with his car. He even has a flashback to watching television the night of his mother's hit-and-run when he was eleven after he looks back to see "Georgina's body lying motionless." At this moment, Chris risks his own life by going back for Georgina's body, and in doing so he's able to rewrite the script of his mother's death, face his demons (even though Georgina ultimately dies in the car), and hopefully heal his deep emotional wounds.

Symbols of Slavery

The screenplay sets the scene of the Armitage home and surrounding property: "The woods give way to a huge clearing. A lovely, medium-sized home sits in the middle. Thick forest surrounds the estate. The property is charming and isolated, no other houses in sight." Though described as a "medium-sized home," it is also described as an "estate" elsewhere in the script, suggesting a larger, more prosperous property. One of the synonyms for the word estate is plantation. This connection becomes painfully more apparent with the introduction of Walter and Georgina, the African American family servants. Dean anticipates Chris' negative reaction by stating that he knows that it "looks bad" having only black servants. But why does it "look bad" — does it resemble a plantation too closely? And by extension, do the servants resemble slaves? Of course, at this point in the narrative, we don't know the full story of Georgina, Walter, or even Andre/Logan. Yet the setting, with its exclusively black staff, creates a world of an isolated Southern estate lost in time.

The iced tea that the Armitages serve and the tea cup that Missy uses to manipulate Chris' mind also harken back to a "gentler" time for plantation owners in the South. Consider Peele's language from his screenplay annotations describing the significance of Andre/Logan's phrasing in his dialogue:

```
ANDRE/LOGAN: My life as an African American
has been, for the most part, very good.
It's hard to be too specific as I haven't
much desired to leave the house in a while.

PHILOMENA: We've become homebodies . . .

ANDRE/LOGAN (to Philomena): But recently,
even when you go to the city. I've just had
no interest. (to the group) The chores are
my sanctuary.
```

The "chores are my sanctuary" suggests that he remains in the house and is happy as a servant. Of course, inside it's just an old white man that likes to do chores for his wife. But in this body, there is a different condition at play — there's the enslavement of the guy's soul involved in having to do that.[13]

Peele's use of the word "enslavement" is key here. His wording reminds us that what we're watching unfold is not just an *Invasion of the Body Snatchers* alien-human relationship but rather a racialized capture that has overtones of subjugation, servitude, and exploitation — all elements of the slave trade. And once we find out that the bodies of Georgina and Walter have been abducted by Rose's grandmother and grandfather, we know what the "enslavement of the soul" really looks like.

---

[13] Peele, *Get Out: The Complete Annotated Screenplay*.

Finally, the scene in which Dean leads the silent auction with a large photo of Chris on an easel next to him is a clear reference to the slave auctions of the antebellum South. In this version, life as a slave would be even worse because both his body and soul would be enslaved. It is also worth noting that Chris' good friend Rod states that he believes that white people want black people only as sex slaves throughout the narrative, a source of humor initially for Chris, the audience, and the police officers, most of whom are African American. However, Rod's belief turns out to be not so far off from the terrible fate from which Chris just barely escapes. And even more striking is the fact that Rod is the only character who explicitly utters the word slave, when clear but unspoken indications of slavery exist throughout the film. Rod's protests are not taken seriously by Chris and are, in fact, played for laughs, as comic relief for the audience because the notion of slavery seems so extreme. However, as we discover, Rod's instincts are spot on, and it is only at the end of the film that we realize how blind we have been to this newly horrific version of enslavement.

Reworking Elements from Classic Films

First and foremost, *Get Out* works as a tightly structured horror suspense film. However, what makes *Get Out* so remarkable is the subtle (or not so subtle) critique of current attitudes of white people about race, and particularly about black people. Jordan Peele has openly stated that his intent while making the film was to provide a racially specific take on the horror genre that would have a profound message about today's current interracial climate.[14] Specifically, the issue of racial anxiety is set up early in the story and intensified throughout using a number of narrative strategies that adapt select plot devices from classic and iconic films.

Jordan Peele has talked about using the similar premise of the 1967 film *Guess Who's Coming to Dinner*, which starred Sidney Poitier, an African American icon of that time. When the protagonist

---

[14] Peele, *Get Out: The Complete Annotated Screenplay*.

Dr. John Prentice expresses concern that his fiancé Joanna has not told her parents that he is black, he is casually assured by Joanna that this fact will not matter to them in the least. In both cases, the women are wrong. In *Guess Who's Coming to Dinner*, Joanna's parents' response is first complete shock, then frustration that their daughter doesn't see the problem, then finally acceptance. In *Get Out*, Chris' reception by Rose's parents is more muted and oddly polite and friendly. In this case, the acceptance occurs almost immediately, but, of course, this is because of a much more sinister agenda.

And yet, Peele's update has some important differences. It turns the situation into a horror story. The very similar set up from *Guess Who's Coming to Dinner* is updated so naturally into a horror story. It's as if it is literalizing the potential for horror that existed in *Guess Who's Coming to Dinner* if things had turned differently.

In *Guess Who's Coming to Dinner*, protagonist Dr. John Prentice and his fiancé Joanna Drayton have not consummated their relationship — a decision made by John, we later learn from Joanna. However, we do see John and Joanna in a passionate kiss through the rear-view mirror of their taxicab (a major criticism of the film at the time). In *Get Out*, we assume that Rose and Chris are involved in a sexual relationship from the beginning of the film due to their playful affection when they are first introduced in the story. The open depiction of an interracial sexual relationship shows how far society has progressed in acceptance of this trend during the nearly fifty years between the films' releases.

Also of note is the talent of our protagonist Chris as a photographer, recalling Joanna, the protagonist in *The Stepford Wives*. The symbolism here is not just characterization through a vocation (in the case of Chris) or avocation (in the case of Joanna); it represents how both main characters are able to see or perceive their situations as vaguely threatening early on. An important difference is that Joanna is seeking artistic validation from a gallery owner, whereas Chris *receives* professional validation from a prominent gallery owner. This difference between the films indicates a level of professional success for our African American protagonist that is notable because it gives him an earned higher-class status that Joanna only receives through her marriage and her race. Of course, though Chris is complemented by gallery owner Jim Hudson, that "admiration" leads to a distinctly horrific attempted theft of Chris' eyes, along with his very soul. The stakes couldn't be higher.

Get Out also parallels *Rosemary's Baby* through its depiction of middle-aged and elderly characters as vaguely odd, leaning toward repulsive, by the very nature of their age in relation to the youth of the protagonists. In *Rosemary's Baby*, the seniors in the building Rosemary and her husband move into are clearly depicted as weird and pushy, while the older folks at the Armitages' party are more quietly creepy and almost always remain within the bounds of politeness and decorum. One encounter at the party crosses that boundary, with a woman asking Rose if sex is better with an African American male while suggestively touching Chris' biceps. The significance of older people depicted in the film *Rosemary's Baby* are as foils to the youth of Rosemary and her husband, while the older people depicted in the film *Get Out* are foils to Chris in terms of both age and race.

Chris attempts to cope with this double-layered alienation and discomfort by reaching out to the black supporting characters Georgina, Walter, and Andre/Logan, who almost all work for the Armitage family as servants. Each encounter with these characters causes Chris to lose hope of making a connection with his racial community while increasing his emotional isolation. Chris' first significant encounter with one of these characters is with the servant Georgina when she pours iced tea for Chris, Rose, and Rose's parents. As Georgina pours the iced tea in Chris' glass, her eyes glaze over, and the script's description states that "subtle flashes of fear cross her face. No one notices" until Chris' glass of tea overflows. Georgina starts to clean and apologizes: "I'm sorry. Look what I've done." Then Missy insists that Georgina leave the spill and rest, and she politely withdraws.

Her apology places her character a world apart from Chris' casual banter with the Armitage parents. Her manner is completely different in an almost identical situation in the film *Guess Who's Coming to Dinner* when Dr. John Prentice sits down for tea with his fiancée and her family. The black maid, Tilly, is openly hostile to John and literally throws a tea cup at him in anger. This is received humorously by both John and the family, but significantly it makes a strong, angry impact so that John knows where he stands with Tilly, who feels he is outside his "proper place" as a Negro in that era.

Only after the disastrous result of his encounter with Andre/Logan, Chris' final attempt to connect with racial community, does Chris finally give up and decide to leave — in part because he can find no solace or camaraderie from any black person that he comes into contact with at the Armitage home. Chris' emotional isolation becomes too much, just as the physical stakes rise even higher with the party guests' auction of Chris. This type of physical and emotional isolation is a key convention in the horror genre. Indeed, Joanna in the influential *Stepford Wives* tries to counteract her isolation by attempting to make friends and even arranging for a "consciousness raising" group for some of the wives in the town. When the meeting is unsuccessful (some of the wives begin to excitedly talk about a household cleaning product), Joanna's emotional isolation intensifies, even with the existence of a female best friend (who she has the most screen time with throughout the film) who never betrays her, though Joanna's husband does. By contrast, Chris has no children, unlike Joanna, or best friend — and no close relationship with anyone nearby at all except for his girlfriend Rose. And we know that Rose eventually and definitively betrays him, just as Joanna's husband betrayed her, with the line, "You know I can't give you the [car] keys." Further, Chris' isolation reads as more intense than Joanna's in some ways since he has no one from his racial group to share the discomfort or alienation that he experiences at the Armitage home, especially since he repeatedly seeks them out to try and control his growing racial anxiety.

Jordan Peele was influenced by earlier horror films, but he doesn't simply duplicate specific sequences without thinking about how a sequence might resonate with a more modern audience. One parallel he incorporates in *Get Out* is to the scene in *Rosemary's Baby* when Rosemary is drugged by the coven in her building (by eating some tainted chocolate pudding) in order for her to be impregnated by Satan. In *Get Out*, Chris is not drugged, but rather hypnotized by Rose's mother, Missy, a therapist, a much more interactive and insidious experience of mind control. In other words, the drugs altered Rosemary's mental state against her will so that she was completely helpless, but her violation was based only on outside forces; Missy, by contrast, deviously elicits and uses Chris' personal childhood trauma from his mother's tragic and violent death as the way to control his emotions and mind. This is more personally invasive. In fact, when it is first suggested that Missy hypnotize Chris to cure him of his smoking habit, Rose rejects this idea, stating, "Believe it or not, some people don't want strangers all up in their heads." Her interaction with Chris much later when he wants to leave uses this same idea.

> CHRIS: I don't know what to say. I think your mom got in my head. I think she got into my head.
>
> ROSE: I thought she helped you.
>
> CHRIS: No, she didn't. She got in my head. She fucked some shit up there and since then . . .
>
> Chris then shuts down.

Peele plays with the fear of psychological violation and violence in Act II first, which then leads to Chris' actual physical danger in Act III.

Critique of Societal Politics

During the prologue, or the opening scene depicting the abduction of Andre, the tone is set for the entire film. This scene presents the distinct difference between suburban spaces (often associated with so-called "white flight" from the city when the white populations in the 1960s and 1970s, especially middle-class and affluent white people, moved from urban neighborhoods undergoing racial integration to the suburbs) and urban spaces (most often associated with black crime and poverty). Peele arranges the dialogue and sense of place in this sequence to clearly challenge the idea that the suburbs are safer than an urban setting, depending on your appearance. Andre, a young black man, is introduced as lost, this seemingly harmless suburban setting an unfamiliar, dangerous space for him. This scene foreshadows our protagonist Chris' later life-threatening predicament at the Armitage estate.

When our film starts in earnest with the introduction of Chris and Rose in Chris' apartment in the city, we are shown how relatively safe the location seems compared to what was shown in the prior scene. The premise of *Get Out* begins with our protagonist Chris packing to spend the weekend at his girlfriend's family home. While he expresses concern that Rose's parents don't know that he is black, he is reassured by Rose that they are "liberal," that her father would have voted for President Obama for a third term if that were possible, and here in his safe space of the city, tying back to the contrast between the city and suburbs, that nod to social politics seems to be enough.

Chris' first encounter with the black groundskeeper, Walter, is during a conversation with Rose's father, Dean Armitage, as the two walk through the grounds that similarly addresses societal norms. The sight of Walter is a distraction to Chris. After noticing Chris' skeptical look at Walter, Dean tries to explain away the fact that his white family has two black servants:

DEAN: I know what you're thinking.

Chris looks at him.

DEAN: White family; Black servants. Total cliché.

> CHRIS: I wasn't gonna go there.
>
> DEAN: You didn't have to. Trust me, I know. We hired them a few years ago to help care for my parents; they're like part of the family now. Couldn't bear to let them go. I hate the way it looks though . . .
>
> CHRIS: Yeah, I know what you mean.

This temporary meeting of the minds between Chris and Dean reflects the so-called "liberal" sensitivity to optics of racial oppression and subjugation. The big tip-off that even this very conversation is only about appearances is Dean's focus on the way things might appear to Chris rather than the "truth" of the situation. In fact, this scene presents us with a double message: Dean is (apparently) sensitive to Chris' feelings, but his explanation that he keeps the black servants, Georgina and Walter, on staff because "they're like part of the family" is a familiar sentiment historically expressed by white slave owners toward their favored house slaves.

The first time Chris actually talks with Walter (moving past their strange but wordless encounter right before Chris is hypnotized by Rose's mother), the script indicates the groundskeeper's demeanor in the following revealing description: "Walter is different than we'd expect. He has a bold and assaulting energy. Like he's concealing a deep loathing with over-the-top enthusiasm. Chilling. Chris is instantly taken aback." We are directed to look beyond an initial appearance of politeness and pleasantness in both Georgina and Walter, and Walter's energy and presentation are even more complex than Georgina's. This is even more apparent when Walter comments about Rose: "One of a kind; top of the line. A real doggone keeper." Walter's dialogue here is filled with casual clichéd and oddly dated phrases, his seemingly appropriate comment expressed with strange phrases that have an old-fashioned or perhaps even simpleminded quality.

Chris' frustrated attempts to connect — or rather, simply communicate — with the African American servants intensify in a second scene with Georgina, who apologizes to Chris for "accidentally" unplugging his cell phone. This leads to an exchange of dialogue between them that both confuses and disturbs at the same time.

> Georgina's voice is shaky and careful.
> Pleasant on top, but angry underneath.
>
> GEORGINA: I owe you an apology. How rude of me to have touched your belongings without asking.
>
> CHRIS: Oh, no. It's cool. I was just confused.
>
> GEORGINA: Just so you know, there was no funny business — allow me to explain. I had lifted your cellular phone this morning in order to wipe down the dresser and it accidentally came undone.
>
> CHRIS: Yeah, I —
>
> GEORGINA: Rather than meddle with it further, I left it that way. How foolish of me.
>
> CHRIS: No. It's fine. I wasn't tryin' to snitch . . .
>
> GEORGINA: Snitch?
>
> CHRIS: Rat you out?
>
> GEORGINA: "Tattletale."
>
> CHRIS: Yeah.
>
> GEORGINA: Don't worry about that. I assure you, I don't answer to anyone.
>
> CHRIS: Right . . . Well, all I know is sometimes, being around too many white people makes me nervous.
>
> He's half joking. Georgina doesn't laugh. Instead eyes get lost for a moment. A tear falls down her face as if there is a pain behind her otherwise vacant smile.
>
> GEORGINA: Oh no, no, no, no, no, no . . .

> Aren't you something? That's not my
> experience. Not at all. The Armitages are
> so good to us; they treat us like family.

Clearly, Georgina, like Walter before her, speaks her own language with a quaint style of dialogue. Her use of the word "tattletale" stands out as both incredibly old-fashioned and at the same time childlike. And her single tear combined with her broad smile is truly frightening as she talks about how the Armitages "treat us like family," cluing the viewer in to the fact that they can't take her statement at face value.

This brings us to the introduction of the character Andre/Logan at the Armitages' party, Chris' last, most explosive, and most revealing encounter with an African American character. In this case, the character is not a servant by trade but rather a more troubling version of an unofficial servant, as seen through his behavior as the scene progresses. Chris' dialogue reveals how much he wants and needs to connect to someone else who is black: "It's good to see another brother around here." But that connection is not to be.

> The man turns to face Chris neatly. It is
> Andre, the jogger from the first scene, but
> he's very different from before. He seems
> glazed-over with the same frozen smile as
> Walter and Georgina.

As Chris continues to try and converse with Andre/Logan, Philomena, described as "60, Caucasian, a stern and guarded wealthy woman," interrupts abruptly and shuttles Andre/Logan away. As a last gesture and show of racial solidarity, Chris offers Andre/Logan a fist bump, to which he responds not with a bump, but by grabbing Chris' fist in an awkward handshake before saying goodbye. Further, the description that follows depicts the nature of Andre/Logan's relationship with both Philomena and the other white party guests.

> Andre/Logan and Philomena laugh and walk
> away. They join a small group of people who

```
applaud Andre/Logan's arrival. Andre/Logan
does a little spin showing off his clothes.
```

This brief performance from Andre/Logan and the fact that he is willingly the entertaining focus of delight for the small crowd of "admirers" clearly depicts the power dynamics in the scene.

Because of how Andre/Logan is introduced, his eventual melt-down is even more striking and disturbing, especially since nothing seemed wrong with him initially. When Chris later tries to surreptitiously take a photo of Andre/Logan with his cell phone to send back to his friend Rod in the city, the flash goes off accidentally. This flash is the catalyst for Andre/Logan to change from what the script terms as "his peaceful expression" to "maddened horror." He moves close to Chris and tensely speaks the titular phrase, "get out." Then, the script states,

```
Andre/Logan grabs Chris by the shoulders and
screams shrilly. Blood trickles out of his
nose.
ANDRE: GET THE FUCK OUT OF HERE!!!!
```

In this moment, Chris finally is confronted with the horror perpetuated at his white girlfriend's family estate, even though the family and Andre/Logan attempt to pass his outburst off as a common seizure afterward. This is the big warning that finally causes Chris to want to leave, a major turning point.

Get Out is a film that works on so many levels — as a horror story, a story of suspense, as well as a story that incorporates the trauma of slavery for black Americans. It is so much more than a standard entry into the horror genre, even though it ticks all the conventional genre boxes. It touches on so many issues with a deft hand of satire and social critique of our current world. And it takes a complex protagonist who proves that he can fight against all types of evil forces and come out on the other side. There's also hope in this story; unlike Joanna's tragic fate in *The Stepford Wives*, Chris survives with his soul intact. Peele has reworked a feminist cautionary tale into a tale of redemption and almost superhuman strength, both mental and physical. The ending of this film proves that it tells not only a story of one man, one character, but also the story of a people overcoming personal trauma and racial oppression.

CHAPTER THREE

Dueling Narratives and Races

in *MUDBOUND* (2017)

> *"I had this thing where I only wanted to work on*
> *original material, no adaptations, and obviously that*
> *changed. I really wanted to have the resources and have*
> *the space and the time to tell stories that I've really cared*
> *about. I've kind of changed my approach, but I've gotten*
> *to do that, to tell stories that I really care about."*
>
> — Dee Rees

In an interview published by Shadow and Act, writer/director Dee Rees discusses what attracted her to the *Mudbound* film project, a story of historical fiction set just before and after World War II that traces a relationship between a white and black family. She also explains her initial thinking about ways to adapt this material and make it her own. After being initially hesitant to work on an adaptation, Rees read the script by Virgil Williams, then was so intrigued that she read the novel by Hillary Jordan on which the script was based. In addition to bringing out the interior dialogue of the characters, the aspect that most interested her about the novel, Rees wanted her version to expand the story of the black Jackson family, and to that end she wanted to bring her personal family history into the script:

> My grandparents, who are from the south, would tell me stories about their younger days, which inspired scenes in *Mudbound* . . . So the project actually inspired me to really dig into my family's history. It presented me with an interesting way to get in touch with my own history and to kind of interrogate it. And so my hope is that the audience feels invited to interrogate their own personal history.[1]

Dee Rees left Nashville for college to study business administration at Florida A&M. In 2003, Rees left a corporate career in marketing. The next year she came out as a lesbian and started making shorts at New York University's graduate film program. Her 2007 thesis short *Pariah* won many awards at film festivals. She wrote a feature script for *Pariah* for the Sundance Institute Screenwriter's Lab and returned the following year for the Directors Lab. This groundbreaking LGBTQ coming-of-age feature film was screened for the first time at the Sundance festival in 2011. It was picked up for release by Focus Features and, ultimately, won an Independent Spirit Award. In spite of all this critical recognition, the next few years were spent developing projects that never got made. Finally, Rees connected with an independent producer at a Women in Film panel who hired her to write and then subsequently got the chance to also direct a biopic on black blues singer Bessie Smith for HBO. In 2015, a producer and Rees' former agent sent a script to her that "touched Rees deeply."[2] That script was *Mudbound*.

Rees liked the Williams script but wanted to rework the story. Rees also wanted to take on the "multiple points of view" that the novel offered, which for the writer/director presented an opportunity to work more conceptually. Although there were challenges involved

---

[1] Tambay Obenson, "A conversation with Dee Rees on 'Mudbound,' her process, influences, genre filmmaking & more," Shadow and Act, September 28, 2017, https://shadowandact.com/dee-rees-Mudbound-conversation.

[2] Anne Thompson, "'Mudbound': Dee Rees, Faith, and the Long Path She Took to Maker Her Epic Oscar Contender," IndieWire, November 13, 2017, https://www.indiewire.com/2017/11/dee-rees-mudbound-director-oscars-netflix-1201895509/.

in such an effort, she felt that the project could say more than "obvious realizations and motivations."[3] Dee Rees felt connected to this project on both a micro and macro level, with the former revolving around her family's personal life experiences and the latter focusing on the important broader issues that the story uniquely presents:

> For me, *Mudbound* is about not being able to come home; it's about family drowning you; it's about the interconnectedness of how we all are, and not just to each other, but also to time.[4]

However, *Mudbound* was not easy to finance. For a period film, the budget of $11.8 million was a challenge, "especially because it had to accommodate the two-day war shoot in Hungary, complete with tanks and airplanes." The remainder of the 26-day shoot was filmed on location in Louisiana. The movie turned out to be 132 minutes long, which was fine with Rees, who wanted to "do an old-fashioned film epic, not whipping through 90 minutes." Ultimately, Netflix bought the movie for more than the $11.8 million budget, and Rees was pleased.[5]

Clearly, Rees found in *Mudbound* a story that she deeply cared about and was able to find herself in, even with all the challenges of its telling and coming to her after being conceived first as a novel and then as someone else's script. The project was seemingly twice removed from the filmmaker, yet it possessed an irresistible opportunity for her to depict a story that became more than the sum of its parts — namely, a unique creation with multiple origins and authors' divergent perspectives.

SYNOPSIS

Jamie and his brother Henry dig a grave for their father, Pappy. It's raining hard and muddy, and Jamie almost gets stuck in the grave until Henry pulls him out. Laura, Henry's

---

[3] Obenson, "A conversation with Dee Rees."
[4] Obenson, "A conversation with Dee Rees."
[5] Thompson, "Dee Rees, Faith, and the Long Path She Took."

wife, walks behind the coffin with their two daughters the next morning. A black family, the Jacksons, drives by in their wagon, and Henry asks them for help even though Laura asks him not to.

The story flashes back to 1939, when Laura in voiceover talks about how she met Henry and how even if she wasn't really in love with him, he made her feel wanted. She also meets his brother Jamie, who is home from college, and who Laura is charmed by and perhaps falls in love with during their first meeting. They dance, and Jamie tries to impress Laura with his knowledge of plays and the finer things. But once Laura accepts Henry's proposal, she settles in to domestic life, which she feels gives her a sense of purpose.

Fast forward to Henry soberly listening to FDR on the radio announcing the attack on Pearl Harbor in 1941. At the same time, we see the Jackson family say goodbye to their oldest son, Ronsel, who goes to fight in the war. Ronsel's mother Florence is heartbroken, but his father Hap becomes more determined to own the land that his family has been working on their whole lives.

Henry tells Laura one day that they will be moving from their comfortable suburban home to a farm in Mississippi. But when they arrive someone else is living in the home, and Henry is told that the man he made the deal with stole his money and left. Pappy, Henry's father, is furious with his son, especially when they must now go and live in a dilapidated house on the farm as a result. The Jackson family dinner is interrupted by Henry demanding that Hap help them unload his truck full of belongings. Pappy and Laura fight over whether she can keep her piano, but she holds her ground and insists that Henry allow it.

Jamie and Ronsel are seen fighting in the war. Jamie is an army pilot, while Ronsel in Belgium writes to his family that his regiment is always on the move. Ronsel's letters talk about how black men are treated better in Europe then back home, and we then see his girlfriend, to whom he is shown bringing flowers.

Back at the farm, Laura's daughters get whooping cough. Florence helps her out and then goes to work for the family even though husband Hap disapproves, not wanting his wife taking care of white children over her own. Both Jamie and Ronsel in the war experience the loss of their fellow soldiers while they manage to survive. Back home, Hap has an accident and breaks his leg. After four weeks, Henry pressures him to return to work in spite of his leg. But Laura takes money from Henry's stash to pay a doctor to take care of Hap. This causes Henry to reject Laura's sexual advances, and even though she didn't always enjoy sex, it made her feel like a wife.

When the war ends both Jamie and Ronsel celebrate with their respective girlfriends. Ronsel and his girlfriend are sad that their relationship is going to end. Jamie returns home and the family is delighted to see him, but there is still tension between Jamie and Pappy over how many men he actually killed. Ronsel's return home involves sitting in the back of the bus on his way home, and he feels as though nothing has changed. He goes to the general store in town to buy some supplies and treats for his family, but when he tries to leave by the front door he is stopped by Henry, Pappy, and another white man, who taunt him. This causes Ronsel to raise his voice in anger, telling the men that black soldiers put their lives on the line killing many Germans and Japanese enemies. But ultimately, he leaves through the back door. Ronsel and his family have an emotional reunion. Later, Henry shows up to tell Hap and Florence what happened at the general store. Hap has Ronsel apologize. After Henry leaves, Hap tells Ronsel that white people always win.

One day after Jamie buys some supplies at the general store he hears a car backfire, which triggers a flashback to the war. Ronsel offers his hand in friendship, which Jamie accepts, offering Ronsel a ride home in his truck. They talk about their experiences in the war, and Ronsel reluctantly accepts Jamie's offer of a drink. They make a toast to their friends lost in the war. When Jamie drops Ronsel off at home, Hap nervously asks Ronsel not to ride with Jamie because there could be trouble for him and the family.

Laura is pregnant again but loses the baby. Florence tries to comfort her by sharing that she also lost a baby of her own. Jamie and Ronsel continue to share war stories together, which worries Ronsel's parents, who think that he might be better off moving to a different place. Jamie admits to Ronsel that his life was saved by black Tuskegee airmen, which is why he feels so close to Ronsel. They also talk about the women they were with during the war, with Ronsel admitting that he had a white girlfriend who wants him to come back to Germany to be with her and their child.

One night, Jamie and Ronsel are seen by Pappy driving around drinking and singing along with the radio. When Jamie gets home, Pappy confronts him about riding with Ronsel and takes the car keys. Jamie starts packing up to leave, and Laura tries to stop him from leaving. She kisses him, and they end up having sex. In the meantime, Ronsel realizes that he lost a letter with a photo of his German girlfriend somewhere along the road where he and Jamie traveled. He goes out into the pouring rain to look for it and is abducted by Pappy and taken to a barn, where he is tied and beaten by members of the KKK. Jamie is brought to the barn to see what they've done to his friend. Horrified, Jamie tries to get the group to set Ronsel free. In response, Pappy and the KKK members force Jamie to decide whether the group will remove Ronsel's eyes, tongue, or testicles. Jamie picks the tongue. Ronsel is left naked and hanging in the barn, where his family finds him. A physically beaten Jamie is dropped of back in bed, bleeding and barely conscious. The next morning Jamie tells Laura that he has killed Pappy by smothering him with a pillow, but Laura tells Henry that Pappy died peacefully in his sleep when he comes home from a trip.

Returning to the opening scene, Hap and Florence drive by with Ronsel secretly hidden in their wagon. Hap helps Henry and, to add insult to injury, is then asked to recite a prayer for Pappy's burial. Hap delivers a prayer filled with anger over the dead man's coffin.

In a city, Jamie walks around in a suit, saying in voiceover that he did not find peace through Pappy's death. Ronsel, meanwhile, returns to the home of his German girlfriend and his son. In voiceover, Ronsel says that he decides to end his story with love.

Revisiting and Revising a Historical Moment

In addition to including the basic elements of fiction (character, dialogue, setting, theme, plot, conflict, and world building) to life, historical fiction has to do so in a way that brings the past to life. Having been adapted from a novel of historical fiction, *Mudbound* had an advantage for the screenwriters in that they did not have to create everything from scratch. However, any successful adaptation must retain (or add, or subtract) elements that work in connection with the requirements of the historical fiction genre.

Having a clear sense of the basic tenets of this genre is essential in order to understand how to approach this type of screenwriting as a whole. M.K. Tod provides an overview of how to think about the basic story elements in the context of historical fiction in the article "7 Elements of Historical Fiction."

Characters, she says, must "behave in keeping with the era they inhabit, even if they push the boundaries. And that means discovering the norms, attitudes, beliefs and expectations of their time and station in life." *Mudbound* takes place in the South during the 1940s, with all the segregation and racism inherent in that region at that time. Though Ronsel and Jamie's uneasy friendship pushes the boundaries of their locale, they are each a product of their particular time, place, and most crucially race.

To convey accurate dialogue, Tod advises authors to "dip occasionally into the vocabulary and grammatical structures of the past by inserting select words and phrases so that a reader knows s/he is in another time period" but not to "weigh the manuscript down or slow the reader's pace with too many such instances." Ronsel, Jamie, and their respective families speak standard English in the film, with special attention given to the spoken accents of the region that writer/director Dee Rees as a Southerner herself could render more authentically.

Tod says that setting, or time and place, is particularly essential in historical fiction, naming "'to bring the past to life' as the primary reason for [viewing] historical fiction . . . Even more critically, you need to transport your readers into the past in the first few [pages]." The first images from *Mudbound*'s script and the novel on which it was based involve the burial of Pappy, Jamie and Henry struggling to dig a grave out of the mud in a pouring rainstorm. This struggle against the elements provides a visual metaphor for the struggles of all the characters who we will come to know to first and foremost work the land that they were given either to own or to work while also creating an immediate connection to the title.

Theme is often difficult to define, and doesn't necessarily apply specifically to one time period: "Most themes transcend history. And yet, theme must still be interpreted within the context of a [screenplay's] time period." The sense of kinship between fellow soldiers and forming bonds across differences are ideas that could be relevant at any time, but these themes gain specificity through the aftereffects of World War II and interracial bonds in a 1950s South both in terms of the individual characters of Ronsel and Jamie as well as the complex and oftentimes painful connections between their two families as a whole.

Plot, of course, "will often be shaped around or by the historical events taking place at that time . . . [but] remember that you are telling a story, not writing history." The entire plot of *Mudbound* and the dramatic trajectory of its protagonists Ronsel and Jamie are completely dependent on their respective (and shared) experiences during the war, yet the intimacy of their story is certainly not one you would find in a history book.

"As with theme and plot," Tod says, "conflict must be realistic for the chosen time and place. [Viewers] will want to understand the reasons for the conflicts you present." Many (though not all) conflicts revolve around racial difference most prominently, with issues of class and gender following less often.

Finally, Tod notes, "You are building a world for your readers; hence the customs, social arrangements, family environment, governments, religious structures, international alliances, military actions, physical geography, layouts of towns and cities, and politics of the time are relevant."[6] Certainly, the physical geography is crucial to the worldbuilding in *Mudbound*, along with the social inequities between white and black people and the violent politics of the time, as manifested through the actions of the Ku Klux Klan.

The sheer number of characters in *Mudbound* who are consequential to the narrative, as well as the relationships between them all, create the major tensions and conflicts at play. Some characters push the boundaries particular to the time period, while others reflect the time's values and attitudes; still others do both. In terms of her writing process, Rees states that typically she "just [writes] it all out on index cards, and just get[s] it all out. It can be scenes. It can be ideas. It can be lines. And it doesn't have to make sense.

---

[6] M.K. Tod, "7 Elements of Historical Fiction," A Writer of History, March 25, 2015, https://awriterofhistory.com/2015/03/24/7-elements-of-historical-fiction/.

And then as you get this floor full of cards, you start to arc them into narratives: Where's this character going? Where's that character going, etc. . . You have to first get it all out, and then shape it and throw away what you need to."[7] But later in the process, Rees explains how disciplined you need to be, especially when managing multiple storylines and characters. She explains how each scene has to work on its own so that you will have stronger sequences, and over the course of the sequences, there needs to be a change or shift in the characters.[8] Rees' method is especially important to note given the daunting nature of an epic historical film project. Her process still involves the basics of screenwriting craft, first letting the creative mind explore the story and only then focusing on creating specific sequences that work as a way to manage multiple storylines and characterizations.

The structure in the book *Mudbound* features a different perspective character from chapter to chapter. This was translated into the script through the use of voice over. Rees mentions how too much voice over risks alienating an audience, and yet this window into the interior world of the characters was one of the major elements that drew her to the project in the first place. As a result, voice over is used throughout the screenplay, but not so often as to take away from the power of the dialogue between characters.

It is also interesting to note who gets to "speak" more often in the novel, as indicated by the number of chapters given to each character. Out of a total of thirty-six chapters, twelve are from Laura's perspective, seven from Jamie's, and four from Henry's, while Ronsel is given five chapters, Florence four, and Hap four. Pappy is the only main character who is not given his own chapter, which makes sense as the story begins with his death. Even more telling is the total number of chapters (twenty-three) from the perspective of the white McAllan family characters compared to the total number of chapters (thirteen) coming from the characters of the black Jackson

---

[7] Obenson, "A conversation with Dee Rees."
[8] Obenson, "A conversation with Dee Rees."

family, a difference of ten chapters. For the film, however, Dee Rees wanted to expand on the Jackson family's story to provide more of a racial balance in the narrative.

One specific change from the novel to the screenplay occurs in the very first scene of the story when, both in the book and the script, Jamie and Henry attempt to bury their father Pappy in the mud-soaked ground. In the midst of digging Pappy's grave, Henry uncovers a skull, skeleton, and finally an iron shackle. The novel has Henry reacting thus:

> "Jesus Christ," Henry said. "This is a slave's grave," . . . "We can't bury our father in a nigger's grave," Henry said. "There's nothing he would have hated more . . ."

The screenplay has Henry using similar words, with a notable exception:

```
HENRY: Jesus. This is a slave's grave . . .
I won't bury our father in a slave's grave.
There's nothing he would've hated more.
```

The substitution of the word "slave" for the word "nigger" is key here. One could argue that Henry's use of the N-word better reflects his father's perspective, as Pappy uses the term with impunity throughout the narrative. And yet, in terms of consistency and audience, the change to "slave" for both instances in the script's dialogue distinguishes the perspective of the son Henry from his father even while Henry tries to honor Pappy's racist views in death. It may seem small or even insignificant to some, but the nuanced change speaks to the effect even one word can have on a scene, especially when the world of the film is being introduced. This adaptation of the dialogue not only signifies a comment on the character's relationships and traits, but also reflects the sensitivities of contemporary audiences, particularly people of color for whom the N-word has had a long and painful history. The N-word is deployed by Pappy and characters with similar racist views in the screenplay (namely members of the KKK), where it retains the most offensive and injurious connotations possible. This shifts the focus away from Henry, who is an antagonist but not necessarily evil, and makes it more about not allowing us to empathize with Pappy, who uses the term all too often.

The element of mud in the first scene and throughout the story reinforces the sense of being stuck, unable to break free. The land itself sucks the viewer back into the past world of struggle with the elements both literally and figuratively, with a major issue being who owns and controls it. Indeed, one of the highlights for the character of Laura is when Jamie constructs a shower for her so that she will have privacy while she bathes away the perpetual grime. Henry's humiliation of losing a house in a deal gone bad is devastating for him and Laura, who fights to hold on to some semblance of her old life through her insistence on keeping her piano. For Laura, the piano symbolizes the connection to her old life in a more genteel and hospitable home, transporting her away from the mud and the grime of their new home as she plays. However, for the Jackson family, owning the land that they work on is both a goal and an elusive dream for Hap, the head of his household. The setting holds both interior and exterior significance.

Dee Rees has said how interconnected the characters are in *Mudbound*, in spite of and emphasized by their separation due to the limitations of the time period. Rees conveys themes that transcend history — how you can't go home again after an experience that changes your worldview, how family can drown you, how true racial equality still seems an elusive aspiration — all in the specific historical context of post–World War II rural South, with all its physical and emotional challenges and dangers. Rees describes the relationship between the McAllan and Jackson families as a kind of "dark symbiosis"[9] — in other words, a mutually dependent arrangement between both parties that benefits no one.

The plot in *Mudbound* is in large part shaped by the historical event of World War II, the catalyst that links the fates of Ronsel

---

[9] Obenson, "A conversation with Dee Rees."

and Jamie in the most dramatic way. This event profoundly changes Jamie's relationship to African Americans in general and Ronsel in particular. It's as if he has suddenly woken up and realized the shared humanity of Ronsel and the Jackson family. However, Jamie and Ronsel are also negatively impacted by their combat experiences during the war. They both suffer from PTSD, and Jamie turns to alcohol as a way to cope.

The major conflicts in *Mudbound* surround not only issues of race, but also gender. The racial transgressions of the Jamie and Ronsel friendship are coupled with the fight for dominance between Laura and her husband Henry. Their marriage is filled with disappointments and resentments; Laura says that Henry is never there when something bad happens. She secretly pays for a doctor's visit when Hap is injured, which so angers Henry when he finds out that he rejects Laura sexually for the first time. At the same time, Laura's growing attraction to Jamie, which had its beginnings at the start of the story, incenses Pappy and confuses Henry.

The world of *Mudbound* exists in the 1930s and '40s in the South, with Laura introducing herself as a 31-year-old virgin; she clearly has deep shame mixed with resignation about becoming a spinster, an old maid, unwanted and without a purpose. Initially, Laura describes her world as very small and has given up hope for marriage and her own family. Laura's first chapter in the novel and first scene in the screenplay introduce not only her character, but also the customs, social arrangements, and family environments that contribute to who the characters are in their own minds and how they navigate the larger world of the story. Laura describes her marriage to Henry as not being passionate or particularly loving, but nevertheless giving her a purpose and a place in the larger society. Clearly, Laura's worldview reflects a bygone era in which women were defined primarily by marriage and children, and her story takes us back into a world where people embraced the limitations assigned by society.

Clearly, the World War II context of the story is used differently in *Mudbound* than other, more iconic interpretations of the war with much of the action on the battlefield, such as *Saving Private Ryan*, through its focus on the U.S. home front and the relationship between two racially different families, the McAllans and the Jacksons. Unique references to the Tuskegee Airmen and sharecropping, as well as broader racial and gender relationships, provide an interesting take specific to the time period.

Dual Protagonists

There is no rule that prevents a screenwriter from writing a story with two protagonists, even though it is difficult enough to create a journey for one protagonist. Hence, it's rarer than one might think to have dual protagonists in a film story. But when it works, it allows us to experience a story and themes from two different perspectives. Some examples of films that successfully utilize the dual protagonist structure include *The Shawshank Redemption*, with Andy's outer, more physical and Red's inner, more psychological journeys; *Thelma and Louise*, both with differing inner journeys; and *Butch Cassidy and the Sundance Kid*, a hero team with different skills that work well together.[10]

In the article "Dual Protagonists: How to Handle TWO Lead Characters in Your Screenplay" from Industrial Scripts,[11] the issues surrounding the creation of more than one protagonist in a screenplay are addressed in great detail. First, we must determine whether *Mudbound*, does indeed have two protagonists, namely Jamie and Ronsel, or rather simply has one protagonist "with a very good, very necessary secondary character."[12] There are a few key elements from the article to determine whether a script narrative actually supports two protagonists.

As the article states, "Dual protagonists must equally spiral, intersect, and clash multiple times throughout the course of your screenplay. Their journeys on both a plot and thematic level have

---

[10] Karel FG Segers, "Why You Should Steer Clear of Dual Protagonists," The Story Department, April 8, 2013, https://www.thestorydepartment.com/dual-protagonists/.

[11] Segers, "Steer Clear of Dual Protagonists."

[12] Industrial Scripts, "Dual Protagonists: How to Handle TWO Lead Characters in your Screenplay," December 20, 2020, https://industrialscripts.com/dual-protagonists/.

to be closely intertwined." One method of crafting dual protagonists is through co-protagonists, or "two characters who both want
the same thing and are both struggling towards the same goal." In
Mudbound, Ronsel and Jamie each have their own journey that is
distinctive, particularly in terms of race, but also similar in terms of
a loss of innocence precipitated by the events of World War II. Each
arc is essential to the overall plot and theme, which is why neither
is simply an important secondary character.

In this way, they function as dual protagonists, and more specifically co-protagonists: "In this method, you have to contrast these
characters so they don't react to conflict in equal ways. They need
to have two very different personalities, which in turn helps high-
light the flaws in both of the characters." Both Jamie and Ronsel
want to find their place in the postwar world after having had clearly
defined roles in the military during the war — Jamie as a fighter
pilot and Ronsel as an army sergeant. They are both lost and trau-
matized when they return home to the same town. They both want
the same thing and struggle toward the same goal, to heal from the
horrors of war that they witnessed and to find a place of acceptance,
comfort, and safety.

However, Jamie and Ronsel are not mirror images of each other,
despite their similar issues and circumstances. They have very different personalities and react to conflict differently, two requirements
of co-protagonists. Jamie uses alcohol to cope with his PTSD and
acts in almost casual defiance of the local white community, while
Ronsel is constrained by the pervasive racist environment and must
put on a "polite" and "respectful" façade in spite of his rage against
the unequal treatment he and his family endure on a daily basis.

"But how do you unify two separate protagonists together?"
asks the article on dual protagonists.[13] *Mudbound* has been called an
ensemble piece. It's also been described as the story of two families,
as well as the story of two men. The film can hold all these elements
because the ultimate force that propels the story to its nearly tragic

---

[13] Industrial Scripts, "Dual Protagonists."

conclusion is the relationship between Jamie and Ronsel, "two veterans — one white and one black — who form an unlikely friendship that unites and divides various members of the community," as the screenplay states.[14]

Despite their differences, Ronsel and Jamie start to form a special bond a little over an hour into the film, beginning with Ronsel reaching out to help Jamie when he reacts to a loud sound in town because of PTSD. After Jamie falls to the ground and drops his groceries in the process, Ronsel literally extends a hand to help Jamie up. Jamie's grateful acceptance of the black man's assistance is looked upon with suspicion by the white spectators, especially after Jamie offers Ronsel a ride home in his truck, but the trauma the men share from the war causes them to journey toward each other. Cowriters Virgil Williams and Dee Rees comment in an article from *Entertainment Weekly* on the covert nature of Jamie and Ronsel's friendship. Rees said, "This is not a straight-ahead relationship . . . It's kind of a queer relationship for me. It's subversive. It's not supposed to be."[15] Rees' reference to queerness as part of the co-protagonists need for their emotionally intense relationship because of their shared wartime trauma creates an implicit intersectionality within their characters and, by extension, the narrative as a whole.

Another significant scene occurring later that solidifies the bond between the two men was not originally in the book. They meet in a barn so that they can talk more freely without family and community listening in. Co-writer Virgil Williams explains: "This scene is decidedly not in the book [by Hillary Jordan]. I need an answer to that question: What happened to Jamie when he was at war? Within that scene, those guys have a forbidden friendship. If you go back and watch it, tracking their scenes, they're not close at all physically. In that barn, they start to get closer and closer to each other."[16] The scene contains a crucial flashback that is part of an

---

[14] Kevin P. Sullivan, "How the *Mudbound* script forged its central relationship," *Entertainment*, February 28, 2018, http://ew.com/movies/2018/02/28/Mudbound-screenplay/.
[15] Sullivan, "The *Mudbound* script."
[16] Sullivan, "The *Mudbound* script."

overall approach in this screenplay that often features two stories in both the past and present:

INT. SAW MILL - DAY - MOMENTS LATER

Jamie and Ronsel shimmy in through a ragged gap. It's old, decrepit and laden with cobwebs. Shafts of sunlight jut in through the wooden slats.

RONSEL: Used to come here when I was a boy. Whenever I needed to be alone and think.

JAMIE: Well I love what you've done with the place.

Jamie offers Ronsel a smoke. Ronsel accepts and Jamie lights his own then tosses Ronsel the lighter. Ronsel lights up and tosses the lighter back.

RONSEL: Why you treating me so nice?

JAMIE: Because you look like you could use it.

RONSEL: Bullshit.

Jamie drags on his smoke and measures Ronsel with a drunken eye. Then:

JAMIE: We were somewhere over Austria and we made contact with a swarm of Messerschmitts. They were everywhere.

HARD CUT TO:

INT. B-25 BOMBER COCKPIT (MOVING) - DAY

It's bumpy as Jamie holds the plane on course. Suddenly bullets rip through the cockpit and the co-pilot gets shredded. Blood splatters on Jamie and on the "LADY LUCK" pin-up girl. Jamie is horrified and we hear his VOICE OVER:

JAMIE (V.O.): Took out my tail gunner, side gunner . . . my co-pilot. Made a deal with God right there. Swore if he saved me I

was gonna do something right. I didn't know
what, but I promised anyway.

BACK TO:

INT. SAW MILL - DAY

JAMIE: Next thing you know, whole bunch
of P-38's show up. Just like the goddamn
cavalry. They knocked those Germans right
outta the sky. I swear they were angels
sent by the Lord himself.

HARD CUT TO:

INT. B-25 BOMBER COCKPIT (MOVING) - DAY

JAMIE (V.O.): Those P-38's, their tails
were painted red. And one of 'em, he buzzed
me after the fight. When I looked over
I thought I was seeing things. But that
fighter pilot? He was colored.

The fighter pilot looks at Jamie and
salutes. Jamie returns the favor. Then the
fighter plane rolls and peels off.

BACK TO:

INT. SAW MILL - DAY

JAMIE: Then he saluted me. And I saluted
back. (beat) Men who died that day . . .
They were fathers. Husbands. Good men. Lot
better than me.

Jamie steeps in his survivor guilt. Ronsel
hands him the bottle and he drinks. They
trade a look, a bond forming.

The scene moves seamlessly back and forth between the wartime
air setting and the present-day sawmill location, not only visually
but also in terms of the use of voice over. In this way, the audience
remains connected to the characters in the present so that this all-
important bond that has developed between these two characters can
perceptibly deepen even as they connect over the past.

A subsequent scene in the same barn location moves the two men even closer emotionally when Ronsel acknowledges his wartime relationship with a German girl. Dee Rees explains about this scene: "It goes further with the next time in the barn with these guys. Jamie asks that deadly question. 'Have you ever been with a white girl?' For me, that felt like a trust fall in a way. If you're uncertain about their friendship, that is the moment where it becomes real, and these guys are keeping each other's secrets in a way."[17]

Two Takes on World War II

The relationships within both families parallel each other, first with the sons, Ronsel and Jamie, and then the wives and mothers, Florence and Laura, and their husbands Hap and Henry. But the symmetry creates an uneasy tension between the McAllan and Jackson families, as the fate of the Jacksons sits squarely at the mercy of the McAllans simply because of their races. In addition to the singular relationship between the co-protagonists Jamie and Ronsel that ties the two families together, each character has strong relationships within their family of origin, and important subplots emerge. For example, danger, both moral and physical, helps define the conflict between Laura and Jamie. Their sexual attraction, affection, betrayal, and finally consummation make up a major subplot. The most prominent conflicts between the characters involve the land, both literally with how difficult it is for Laura to physically keep clean in such a hostile environment (foregrounded in the title *Mudbound*) and figuratively for Henry in terms of ownership, particularly his failed deal for a house that forces them back to the rundown farm. Pappy, the patriarch of the McAllan clan, is the most threatening antagonist and bully to Jamie and Laura, and he intimidates Henry even after his death.

In addition to the main characters' strong connections to their respective families are the internal emotional mechanisms within each family and the racially defined allegiances to their respective

---

[17] Sullivan, "The *Mudbound* script."

communities. The McAllan family is characterized by an inability to emotionally connect with each other. They are essentially a broken family. They move through a cycle of missed opportunities for intimacy throughout the narrative. Jamie, in particular, suffers from an inability to openly express his feelings of kinship toward Ronsel or his attraction to Laura. He is constantly thwarted in his many attempts to connect to both throughout because of the taboo nature of each relationship. Henry unsuccessfully attempts to keep control of Laura, both in the role of her husband, arguing about allowing her piano, and also through his father, when Pappy brazenly walks past Laura while she is bathing outside the house without privacy. However, when the male McAllan family members connect with the larger white community, it is through intimidation, as seen with Pappy and the others in the grocery store threatening Ronsel or with Henry when he subsequently demands that Ronsel apologize to Pappy for his actions at the store. And in the end, Pappy unifies the larger white community, including the KKK, in acts of violence and terror against both his son Jamie and Ronsel. As patriarch of the McAllan family, Pappy violates (either physically or emotionally) every member of his kin before ultimately meeting his end at the hands of Jamie, his younger son, who finds the courage to rise up against him.

On the other hand, the Jackson family relationships are primarily loving, if tense at times. The conflicts between the patriarch Hap and his family stem from his frustration at not being able to buy the land that he works on or protect his wife Florence from exploitation as a caretaker of the McAllan family or help his son adjust to postwar life. Hap is shown as a leader in his church, and the church services show the larger black community as unified through their faith. Even in the worst of circumstances, Hap holds on to his faith, especially evident when he is forced to help bury Pappy (when on his way out of town with his family) and say a prayer for him that is unexpectedly strong and forceful. The contrasts between the white and black communities that each family is a part of are striking, with the rural black community characterized as unified in faith while the rural white community is effectively mobilized through the poison of racism. This is most explicit and terrifying when Jamie is presented with a dilemma where he is forced to make a choice between two equally bad alternatives in the planned mutilation of Ronsel.

In the end, we are left with an overall circular structure of the story, neatly concluding where it started. We don't completely understand the opening flash-forward introduction of Jamie and Henry struggling to bury their father until we revisit the same scene later, only now with the knowledge of all that we have witnessed throughout the film. We've narratively traveled a full circle, but at a shocking and gruesome human cost.

Mudbound is not always easy to accept, but it successfully transports us to another time and place and addresses so many racial issues that still persist to this day. However, the hope is that if we have the courage to look at our shared, often dark past, then we can create a present and future that we can all experience with pride and joy. As Dee Rees states, "I think the film will make people connect with the now. People dismiss bad behavior and say, 'well, he's a man of his time,' My point is, we make the times. We are the times."

Embracing Inclusive Collaboration in the Creative Process

The novel that *Mudbound* is based on is by a white female author, Hillary Jordan. The first draft of the screenplay was written by Virgil Williams, a black man, and the final draft was written by Williams in collaboration with the African American female writer/director Dee Rees. I describe all the authors in this way to address a concern that many screenwriters/filmmakers have that we also discussed regarding *Moonlight*: Namely, who is allowed to tell whose story? *Mudbound* contains a multitude of elements dealing with race, gender, class — it has it all! The characters are all over the map, but in the simplest terms, we have a white family and a black family. Should a white author only write about white people, or, conversely, should black writers only create black characters and black narratives? What if there's a mix or combination of characters of different races, as in *Mudbound*? There are no easy answers here; however, the case of *Mudbound* can serve as one model of how to successfully collaborate across racial and gender lines.

I view the creative process of bringing *Mudbound* to the screen as a relay race, where the book's author runs the first leg of the race, the first screenwriter the second leg, and the director takes the final stretch to cross the finish line. You couldn't run the race by missing any members of the team. It's a group effort — which is why the relay is one of my favorite types of races to watch. The coordination, the timing, the full-out effort on every leg of the race by each individual runner is a wonder to behold. So, too, is a successful collaboration to bring a powerful story to the screen. The process of adaptation and collaboration is rarely easy and never without any conflict, especially when representations of race are involved. But a team that is in some meaningful way representative of the story being told is a good start.

I believe *Mudbound* is a very successful screenplay in large part because of the creative decisions that were made to give the Jackson family an expanded storyline of greater depth. In addition, the ending in the film, when Ronsel returns to Germany to be with his wartime love Resl and his young son, brings a welcome dose of resilience and agency to his character, whereas in the novel the ending is more ambiguous. Co-screenwriter Virgil William addresses this change in an interview, explaining why he felt so strongly that he had to provide a more definitive and hopeful ending in the script:

> What's just more important in a movie than a novel is to leave people in a state of feeling; for me, a film is really made in the language of emotion. And in that book, Hillary [Jordan], she was upset when I told her I was going to change her ending, [which] just alludes to the possibility of what Ronsel could potentially be and where he could potentially go. And I didn't think that was a satisfying enough ending.
>
> And part of that is that I'm a minority, and, quite frankly, there are too many fatherless black children in the world. For Ronsel to truly occupy the space of a hero, he needed to go get his son. It is

the very reason he got his tongue cut out and if he didn't fulfill that relationship, it would have felt very non-cinematic and, quite frankly, not satisfying at all. And, after all that pure truth in the movie, after all that searing idea of America, you really need to end on a hopeful note. *Mudbound*, I hope, shows us who we were and, in doing that, it shows us who we are and on that hopeful note will inform who we choose to be.[18]

---

[18] Andrew Karpan, "Why Virgil Williams Changed the Ending to 'Mudbound,'" FSR, November 27, 2017, https://filmschoolrejects.com/virgil-williams-changed-ending-mudbound/.

CHAPTER FOUR

Memories of Childhood Revisited

in *ROMA* (2018)

> *"I said it was going to be a film that nobody would see . . .*
> *But it's been a really moving, strange process, finding the way*
> *people are responding . . . And it's almost overwhelming. I didn't*
> *calculate that people would find [something so personal, so*
> *universal]. I wish I could calculate those things."*
>
> — Alfonso Cuarón

Roma has been hailed as a masterpiece. It's also been the subject of controversy because of the many issues that emerged during the course of Cuarón's seemingly very personal semi-autobiographical film about the character of Cleo, a middle-class Mexican family's live-in maid and nanny (who is based on Cuarón's real-life nanny, Libo, to whom the film is dedicated):

> The different ways of perceiving its representation of Mexican history, and race and class relations, have generated debates about racism, privilege, power, empathy, and compassion . . . *Roma's* profuse reception by the press and on social networks, as well as its adoption by the Mexican women's rights nonprofit . . . organizing for the rights of

domestic workers in the United States, Mexico, Ecuador, and Colombia . . . proves its global reach.[1]

One might ask: How could a relatively small-scale story, essentially a memoir of sorts, generate so much critical attention and numerous awards about its subject matter on an international scale? For one, *Roma* can be said to be Netflix's entry into the prestige project arena, with much-celebrated writer/director Alfonso Cuarón, whose credits include *Gravity* (2013), *Children of Men* (2006), and *Y Tu Mama Tambien* (2001), helming the project. On the other hand, part of the answer to that question might lie in the fact that domestic workers are rarely the protagonists of dramatic feature films. The fact that this group has been so underrepresented in films was a catalyst for both celebration and activism simultaneously.

Alfonso Cuarón is a Mexican director and screenwriter who has an international reputation for powerful storytelling in a wide range of genres. Cuarón studied film at the Centro Universitario de Estudios Cinematograficos (a school within the National Autonomous University of Mexico) but was expelled due to his creating and shooting a film in English instead Spanish as part of a school project. But Cuarón found work as a technician in Mexican television, then as a television director, and finally as a movie director. Cuarón's first feature film, for which he also wrote the screenplay, was *Solo con tu pareja*, or "Love in the Time of Hysteria," in 1991. The American director Sydney Pollack, after seeing this film, offered him a chance to direct a television episode for his series *Fallen Angels*. Two English language theatrical films followed: *A Little Princess* in 1995 and *Great Expectations* in 1998. However, Cuarón's breakout film came when he returned to Spanish language filmmaking. *Y Tu Mama Tambien*, or "And Your Mother Too," which he also wrote, is a 2001 film about a road trip with teenage boys and an attractive married woman that was nominated for Best Original Screenplay at the Academy Awards in part because of its commentary on social class

[1] Sergio de la Mora, "Roma: Repatriation vs. Exploitation," *Film Quarterly*, June 7, 2019, https://film-quarterly.org/2019/06/07/roma-repatriation-vs-exploitation/.

within Mexico. During this period, Cuarón also became identified with fellow filmmakers Guillermo del Toro and Alejandro González Iñárritu as part of a new wave of Mexican cinema. Cuarón returned to English language films with *Harry Potter and the Prisoner of Azkaban* in 2004 and *Children of Men* in 2006. In 2013 he cowrote and directed *Gravity,* for which he won an Academy Award for Best Director. And then he followed these large-scale films with a highly personal memoir based on his family life in 1970s Mexico City.[2]

In addition to the subject matter, the film's painstaking production design to recreate Cuarón's 1970s memories is memorialized in the documentary *Road to Roma* (2020). The original screenplay by Cuarón, which was nominated for an Academy Award, reflects an incredibly complex and multifaceted approach to filmmaking that is anything but conventional.

SYNOPSIS

In 1970s Mexico City, Cleo, a young housekeeper, works for an upper middle-class family. She takes care of four children, Toño, Paco, Pepe, and Sofi, and their parents, Antonio and Sofía, who don't get along very well. In fact, Antonio is often away on business trips. One day, he leaves for an extended trip to Canada. While Sofía begs him to stay, hugging him tightly, he pulls away and leaves anyway.

Cleo's boyfriend is named Fermin, the cousin of her fellow housekeeper Adele. When Adele, Adele's boyfriend Ramon, Fermin, and Cleo go on a double date to the movies, Fermin and Cleo steal away to a hotel room. He tells her he loves her, but when she later discovers that she is pregnant, he abandons her at a movie theater. Cleo then tells Sofía about the pregnancy, crying because she's afraid

---

[2] The Editors of Encyclopaedia Britannica, "Alfonso Cuarón," *Encyclopedia Britannica,* accessed November 1, 2021, https://www.britannica.com/biography/Alfonso-Cuarón.

of being fired. But instead firing her, Sofía takes her to a doctor who confirms her pregnancy.

For Christmas and New Year's, the family goes to Sofía's brother's estate. During the New Year's celebration Cleo sees a man hitting on Sofía, who rebuffs him, stating that she is a married woman. The celebration is interrupted by a massive fire that all the guests try to put out.

Back at home, Cleo asks Ramon where Fermin is, and he reluctantly tells her. She travels with Ramon out to a martial arts training camp. But when Cleo tries to tell Fermin that the baby is his, he threatens to become physically violent if she ever tries to find him again. Teresa, Sofía's mother who also lives with the family, takes Cleo shopping for a crib, and they run into a student protest that turns violent. While still in the store, Cleo sees Fermin as a member of the protest. Cleo is stunned by this, and her water breaks. Teresa rushes Cleo to the hospital, but despite the doctor's efforts Cleo's baby is stillborn.

Depressed, Cleo returns to work, and Sofía invites Cleo on a family weekend trip to the beach as a guest, not an employee. When they get to the beach town, Sofía tells the children at dinner that their father is not coming back home, that in fact this trip to the beach was planned so that he could take his things from the house without seeing the family. The children are upset, but Sofía puts on a brave face, telling them that this will be an adventure and that she is quitting her job as a professor to start a new career in publishing. At the beach, Sofía leaves for a moment with Toño while Paco and Sofía go in the water to swim. Sofía warns them to stay in the shallow water because Cleo can't swim. But while Cleo is distracted taking care of Pepe, she realizes that she cannot see the other two children. Cleo bravely walks out to them through strong waves that nearly knock her down. And even though she cannot swim, Cleo successfully rescues the children from being pulled out to sea by the currents. The whole family embraces in relief while the children declare to their mother "Cleo saved us. Cleo saved us." Then Cleo begins to cry and confesses that she never wanted her baby that was stillborn and that she is filled with guilt. The family comforts her in a group, hugging each other tightly.

Back at home, the house is a bit emptier since Antonio took not only his books, but also the bookcases and other prized possessions. Then the family and Cleo begin the adjustment to their new environment, with everyone falling back into their usual routine.

Short Story Structure

Often when we think of dramatic structure, we think of the traditional three-act structure and a protagonist who is actively seeking their wants and needs, which keeps the plot moving. However, the way the narrative in *Roma* unfolds is not completely straightforward but rather something different, something more. In the article "Alfonso Cuarón's *Roma*: A Short Story Captured on Film," Catharine Romero-Perla suggests that the narrative plays out in a manner more similar to a short story than a typical film with a clear three-act structure. She states, "The result is a short story film adaptation with no short story to accompany it — it is simply a short story captured on film."[3] Romero-Perla specifically identifies three aspects that make *Roma* a short story in her view: "the use of third objective, the personal as universal, and the epiphany."

> A quick google search defines 3rd objective as, "a narrator who tells a story without describing any thoughts, opinions, or feelings." Which begs the question, why would anyone choose this perspective if it doesn't offer any interiority from a character? *On Writing Short Stories*

---

[3] Catharine Romero-Perla, "Alfonso Cuarón's 'Roma': A Short Story Captured on Film," Medium, February 25, 2019, http://c-romperla.medium.com/alfonso-cuar%C3%B3ns-roma-a-short-story-captured-on-film-93fcd39c375.

suggests 3rd objective forces the audience to pay attention to a character's dialogue and actions in order to understand them.

In many ways, the third objective reflects the real world. For instance, if we're in line ordering coffee and the person in front of us has a special order, is rude, or takes too long, we will make a conclusion of that person based on the way they spoke and the choices they made. This is how the third objective works. Through our observations, we can begin to understand them.[4]

Romero-Perla also sees short stories as having a unique ability to capture something so personal that it resonates as something far greater, far more, than what the story is ostensibly about:

> Short stories have the power to be universally understood. Regardless of the readers own experience and background a story well-crafted and well-written will resonate across all languages — across all cultures.[5]

Finally, Romero-Perla draws attention to the epiphany at the climactic moment in *Roma*. The epiphany in a short story, she says, comes from James Joyce:

> Although the definition remains somewhat obscure . . . one of his characters states, "epiphanies are a sudden and momentary showing forth or disclosure of one's authentic inner self. This disclosure might manifest itself in vulgarities of speech, or gestures, or memorable phases of the mind."[6]

It should be noted that the significant cinematic movement Italian neorealism, which began in the 1940s postwar period, also meets these three criteria of this "short story" through its focus on the everyday routines of common people (as in the film *Bicycle Thieves*, for example). Italian neorealism features a mix of professional and non-professional actors, location shooting, improvised dialogue, and a lack of moral censorship, all of which are evident in *Roma*. So while the use of these three aspects is not completely new to film,

---

[4] Romero-Perla, "A Short Story Captured on Film."
[5] Romero-Perla, "A Short Story Captured on Film."
[6] Romero-Perla, "A Short Story Captured on Film."

they are utilized effectively and prominently in *Roma*, giving us a combination of the unusual structure and a more U.S.-based audience through Netflix.

If we think of the significant dramatic moments in *Roma*, Cleo's character comes across as a bit of a mystery. She reacts, but we aren't given direct access to her internal or emotional life as we are to Señora Sofía her employer; actually, we mainly see Cleo moving, moving, moving, as she works virtually nonstop in her household. So we are left as observers, who look instead for subtle choices that the character makes, something as basic as whether to speak or stay silent at a given moment in addition to what is spoken, for example, or perhaps physical gestures and actions that reveal an emotional response to a specific situation or dramatic moment. For Cleo, the first such moment comes early in the story when the family is enjoying a comedy show on television and, though she begins by serving dessert while collecting the soiled plates of dinner, she joins them. She is transfixed by the show and, as the screenplay describes, "sets aside the plates and sits down on the floor next to the sofa to watch T.V." It's as if she forgets that she is the maid, but rather becomes one of the family, as two of the children reach to hug her after she sits. However, a moment later, Señora Sofía tells Cleo to bring Señor Antonio some chamomile tea. Cleo responds immediately with a "yes, ma'am," picks up the plates from the floor, and heads downstairs to get the tea.

This scene is one of the only ones in which Cleo takes the liberty of stopping in the middle of her seemingly nonstop chores to join in the family fun. Even at this early stage, the audience wonders what exactly Cleo's relationship to this family really is. Of course, we know that she's officially the hired help, but it seems like more, especially after the television show incident. And yet, she is reminded of her "official" role almost immediately by Señora Sofía. The intimacy of that moment with the family is short lived and ends abruptly. Throughout the film, this dynamic between Cleo's official role as housekeeper, nanny, and employee and her unofficial one as special member of the family shifts back and forth uneasily in a way that, despite Cleo's distinctly subservient manner, suggests something stronger and deeper existing within her character.

Though *Roma* is focused on the specific life of Cleo's character, an early scene on a rooftop in which Cleo tends to the family's clothes that have been hung out to dry suggests that aspects of her story and situation are more universal. This is indicated through the following visual description, written in the screenplay and translated directly to the screen:

```
The afternoon quiet hours have begun. Church
bells ring in the distance. All around
them, a landscape of roofs mushrooming in
all directions. In many of them, other
women wash or hang laundry. The wind
carries the hum of different radios and
dogs barking. The whistle of a sweet potato
cart. The quiet universe.
```

Cuarón brings the labor of domestic workers into sharp focus in a powerful way by opening up space for them, starting on the script page to include those women in addition to Cleo who, while nameless and faceless, still matter and are acknowledged in this moment. In this way, Cuarón's personal story becomes more universal, encompassing the large group of domestic workers who usually go unseen by not only this family of characters in Mexico City, but potentially all over the world, wherever domestic workers exist.

Finally, near the end of film, Cleo's epiphany is clear and heartbreaking, occurring on the beach after she has saved two of her employer's children from drowning while risking her own safety. She has been quietly enduring not only the demands of her employer's family, but her own private journey with her ill-fated pregnancy. Suddenly, the floodgates open from deep within Cleo:

```
SOFI: Cleo saved us . . .

The recent emotion pushes more tears.
Señora Sofía looks at Cleo, who is crying
```

inconsolably. It is a deep and painful cry, a cry that washes it all away.

Señora Sofía hugs her mightily —

SEÑORA SOFÍA: Thank you, thank you, thank you Cleo . . .

But Cleo can't stop crying —

CLEO: I didn't want her . . . I didn't want her . . .

Señora Sofía tries to calm her —

SEÑORA SOFÍA: Shhh, shhh, shhh . . . They're OK. The kids are OK . . .

But Cleo insists amidst tears and snot —

CLEO: I didn't want her . . . I didn't want her to be born . . .

She breaks down completely —

CLEO: Poor little girl! . . . I didn't want her to be born! . . . I didn't want her to be born! . . .

SEÑORA SOFÍA: It's going to be all right, Cleo . . . It's going to be all right . . .

The two women cry, hugging. It's a shared cry, with sobs like retching, and long silences exploding in prolonged vocals.

The children close in on the women, hugging them. Only Toño watches, standing by.

The onlookers scatter. The rider pulls the reins and the horse continues its way down the beach.

The furious sea and its restless waves reflect the last glimmers of the day.

The description and dialogue in the final product may be different in the screenplay. Cuarón has stated that he never showed the cast the full script; the writer/director would just give them a few pages at a time, set up the scene and situation, and then let the camera roll. When such a choice is intentional, it's fine that some elements of the scene are not on the page. In this way, the use of the script is more of a sketch than a specific blueprint for the film. Indeed, collaboration between the cast and writer/director, built from what is on the page, creates an authenticity, a level of craft that relies heavily on the experience of the writer/director — not just the professional, more so the personal experience. This tends to be the process of writer/directors. Thus, the dialogue and description in the beach scene differ from the final filmed version, but the essence of the scene remains the same. Indeed, Cleo's epiphany is extremely well motivated, painfully realizing that she didn't want her own biological child just after she risked her life for her employer's children. Her admission verbalizes her sense of guilt, as well as reflecting a side of her own character that has an essential need for the family that she serves. This is a complex moment for Cleo and the audience, who has seen her only as the nurturing and mostly silent force in the household that she essentially holds together through her many domestic roles as caretaker. While the decision of the baby's death was made for her, this voluntary admission speaks volumes about Cleo's overwhelming need for her place in her employer's family, which supersedes even her desire for her own family.

This short story structure effectively works to build to this stunning epiphany because we as an audience have had Cleo's internal emotional life mostly withheld from us. Our understanding is based almost totally on observed behavior within the context of a specific yet universal story world, and her epiphany shatters that emotional distance.

Class, Gender, and Systemic Racism

Alfonso Cuarón has said about Cleo's characterization that she has three strikes against her in the social hierarchy: her class, race, and gender. But Cuarón's perspective in the film, Sergio de la Mora of Film Quarterly states, seems to acknowledge "that he and other middle-class Mexicans enjoy lives that are built on the exploitation of poor Indigenous or mestiza women . . . By placing value on her story, Cuarón is giving back to Libo — and all the other Cleos of the world." Even more directly, Cuarón admits, "It was probably my own guilt about social dynamics, class dynamics, racial dynamics . . . I was a white, middle-class Mexican kid living in this bubble. I didn't have an awareness."[7]

In spite of his perspective from a place of privilege, Cuarón depicts clear, primarily negative patriarchal forces at work both in the home, with head of the household Señor Antonio, and outside of it, with Fermín. These two characters abandon their relationships almost simultaneously in the narrative, so that by the time Cleo tentatively approaches Señora Sofía about her pregnancy, both Señor Antonio and Fermín have departed in some way. Through their actions, Cuarón creates a dramatic parallel between Cleo and Señora Sofía that transcends class and comments more broadly on gender relationships.

Overall, the depictions of the male characters in the film are less than flattering. Their actions are framed as self-absorbed, unreliable, violent, and macho in relation to the women in their lives. Señor Antonio, a doctor who insists on having a car that is too large for his small courtyard, reflects a superficial focus that renders him almost absurd when he parks the car with such extreme care in the scene in which he is introduced, forming our first and perhaps strongest impression of him. As he heads out for his so-called conference trip, he carries a couple of large suitcases before Cleo quickly takes them and heads out to the waiting car. Señor Antonio thanks Cleo, ironic coming from a large man who would willingly hand over two heavy suitcases to someone so much smaller than him. This subtle but telling action shows how Cleo is the actual strength of the household in every conceivable way. The scene in which Señor Antonio is grabbed desperately from behind by Señora Sofía is heartbreaking, as it's clear that the doctor can't wait to leave his loving wife

---

[7] De la Mora, "Roma: Repatriation vs. Exploitation."

and family. Señor Antonio comes across as cold and rejecting, but we see no evidence as to why.

The final two times that we see Señor Antonio, he is first frolicking with some woman on a busy street, oblivious to the fact that one of his sons has seen him. And then we see him with his empty words of support at the hospital when Cleo is about to deliver her baby. Overall, Señor Antonio is depicted as self-absorbed and unreliable, even hurtful, especially when he arranges to take all of the bookshelves from the house after he has moved out while the rest of the family is on their trip near the end of the film. This final impression of Señor Antonio's presence is of him as a taker and not a giver, still absorbed with material things such as the bookcases and his car over his family.

Fermin, Cleo's boyfriend, seems nice and considerate when we first meet him. However, when we see him in the hotel room where he and Cleo have sex, he puts on a martial arts display that is meant to impress her, but actually comes across as a somewhat comical macho show of physical prowess. This performance of physical strength becomes more serious when Cleo finds Fermin to tell him of her pregnancy; he threatens her with violence, so now that strength would be used against her. This is already a 180-degree shift from the way things first started with their relationship. And if that weren't enough, later Fermin is armed with a gun as part of a violent protest at a department store where others have been shot. Though he backs away after he sees Cleo, she is so shaken by the change in him that her water breaks. Fermin moves from a martial artist to associating with killers. He becomes violence incarnate during the course of the narrative.

The Supporting Role in the Family Becomes the Lead

Roma is distinctive for placing someone in the role of servant as the protagonist in the film. The character of Cleo is front and center in the narrative. She is given the most screen time, and the development of her character is measured and nuanced, when traditionally the maid in a film is represented as a one-dimensional caricature and lives at the margins of the plot. However, *Roma* is not the only film that has dramatized this subject recently in Latin America, but rather part of a larger trend. Sergio de la Mora in *Film Quarterly* states:

> *Roma* is part of distinct trend in contemporary Latin American cinema: stories of domestic workers, servants, and their masters, many of them made by women directors. A host of films explore the servant-employer relation, including *La Cienaga* (Lucrecia Martel, 2001), from Argentina, in which the director shows how clearly all the family members project onto the maid their fears and desires, appreciation, paranoia, and obsessions . . .
>
> In Mexican cinema, female domestic workers tend to be portrayed as comical and gossipy or as erotic objects, or they remain marginalized in the narrative.[8]

As part of this more recent trend, in *Roma*, Cleo is portrayed as none of those things exclusively. Yes, she does listen to gossip with her fellow domestic worker Adela, but she is not depicted as obsessively gossipy. Cleo is also shown being sexual, which makes her human in the film's context and not at all objectified. And what is also clear is that Cuarón emphasizes the intersection between race and gender by casting an indigenous actor, Yalitza Aparicio, as the indigenous domestic character Cleo, as it is rare to see indigenous actors in any significant role in high profile films from any country. The simple description of her character in the screenplay states "a Mixtec indigenous woman," which conjures up a host of visuals — darker skin, smaller frame, distinctive facial features and hair texture. This contrasts with the "white" Mexican family that she serves and reflects a visual representation of a racial hierarchy inside and outside of Cleo's household. The specificity of the character is also a comment on the racialized and gendered nature of the domestic help in Mexico (and elsewhere). A specific description and its relationship to casting is essential to the nature of the subject matter of the narrative. Again, there is an honesty in the casting, an intentionality that purposely does not cast established stars and lends a

---

[8] De la Mora, "Roma: Repatriation vs. Exploitation."

greater authenticity to our main character Cleo, but that also relies upon the considerable experience of Cuarón to bring out the best performances.

Yet the question remains: What is Cuarón's approach to Cleo's character as racially and culturally subjugated relative to others, while nevertheless as the center of the narrative? And how does the writer/director authentically represent a vivid and compelling portrayal of an often timid and submissive protagonist? The nature of Cleo's character is not of a typically active protagonist; rather, she is essentially reactive. Yet she is definitely not passive, as has been suggested by some analysts of the film. Novelist K.M. Weiland offers a useful explanation of the difference on her website Helping Writers Become Authors. While Weiland's advice is aimed primarily at book authors, it can easily be applied to screenwriters as well. Weiland makes a critical distinction between a reactive and passive protagonist and why the former can work well, while the latter is something to be avoided at all costs. The reactive protagonist, Weiland says, is:

> Off-Balance: The First Plot Point is something that comes along and physically *smacks* the protagonist. It literally knocks her off-balance. Some First Plot Points might fling her completely off her feet; others might only make her trip. But she's shaken up. She's scrambling to not just regain her feet, but to figure out what just hit her. She's *reacting*. She's not the one who did the hitting; she's the one who *got* hit. And now she has to compensate in some way.

Cleo is initially knocked "off-balance" when she realizes that she's pregnant. She is the one who gets hit with the primary responsibility for her unplanned pregnancy, and she is completely shaken to her core. Basically, Cleo spends the rest of the film trying to manage the consequences that come from this change.

> Not in Control of the Conflict: Her reactivity is almost solely the result of the fact that she is not the one who is controlling the conflict. The antagonistic force is firmly in control at this point. Stuff is happening to the protagonist, and she can't stop it. She can't even properly combat it, because her balance is compromised.

As a reactive protagonist, Cleo is not in control of the conflict between herself and boyfriend Fermin, who, as the antagonist, is firmly in control of what he's doing and his choices. By contrast, Cleo can't stop him or affect the outcome of the conflict in any way. This stage of her character's development culminates when Fermin abandons her at the movie theater after she's told him that she's pregnant.

> Not in Possession of a Complete Understanding of the Conflict and the Antagonistic Force: Not only is the protagonist not in control of the conflict, but she doesn't even fully *comprehend* the conflict. She may not understand what's happening to her *at all* or even how it might be possible. At the least, she doesn't understand why the antagonist is getting in her way or what the antagonist's motives may be.

The next phase also involves Fermin. Cleo does not understand him, or even the nature of the conflict between them. And because she does not understand enough about the conflict, she can't anticipate what Fermin's next move will be. This conflict resolves with Fermin threatening physical harm if Cleo tries to find him again, and he walks away for a second time.

> Not in Possession of a Complete Understanding of Himself and His Own Motives: His blindness about himself, just as much as is any other factor, is causing him to get smacked around during this part of the story.

Cleo's character moves through the stage of understanding herself and her own motives, significant because she struggles to understand during most of the story. That is why the scene at the beach where Cleo confesses that she didn't want her baby is so significant. Her words reflect the insight into herself that she's gained in increments over the course of the narrative. It is an explosive and emotional moment and, in many ways, the most important dialogue that we hear in the film.

By contrast, Weiland notes a number of things that a reactive protagonist like Cleo is not:

- **Passive:** Just because a protagonist is reacting doesn't mean she's passive.

- **Goal-less:** Your protagonist may be reacting — she may not be in control of the conflict — she may not fully understand what's going on. But she still wants something. She has a goal and she's moving toward it, or at least *protecting* her ability to move toward it later.
- **Stupid:** We sometimes equate passivity with stupidity. But a reactive character *is* doing something: she's trying to regain her feet, she's trying to shield herself from the rocks. And even if she's not being too successful at it yet, that's most definitely *not* stupid.
- **Defeated:** Passivity is also often equated with defeat. But your character is reacting, she's not passive, and she's definitely not defeated.[9]

To recap, Cleo always has goals, though mainly through her pursuit of Fermin taking responsibility for her pregnancy, so she is not a passive character. Yes, her character was dependent on others, with Señora Sofía finding a doctor for the pregnancy and the grandmother, Señora Teresa, looking for baby cribs, but Cleo is not stupid or helpless; she is always trying to regain her balance, from the very beginning. Cleo has a big off-balance moment when she sees Fermin in the department store and her water breaks. But she is certainly not defeated, as she survives not only her unplanned childbirth but also her rescue of Sofi and Paco. The fact that neither she nor the children drown in her rescue attempt makes her doubly successful and shows her courage. At the end of the day, though Cleo may seem timid and reticent to get involved (in a word, passive), she is in fact reactive, pushing through and pushing back on everything that happens to her.

Colonia Roma in Mexico City

Cuarón's attention to detail on this film is legendary in the world of cinema, particularly in terms of setting. The house is situated in the Colonia Roma neighborhood of Mexico City, and the façade was recreated as a duplicate of Cuarón's home during the 1970s from specific

---

[9] K.M. Weiland, "A Reactive Protagonist Doesn't Have to Be a Passive Protagonist! Discover the Difference," Helping Writers Become Authors, May 31, 2015, https://www.helpingwritersbecomeauthors.com/passive-protagonist/.

descriptions in the screenplay. In the Netflix documentary *Road to Roma*, Cuarón discusses how accurate to his boyhood experience the setting and props needed to be to get the authentic feeling that he wanted for the film. For example, the screenplay includes specific descriptions of the special world of the film, closely referencing his real-life boyhood home with as much meticulous attention to each area of the house as he could, based on his memories. One scene in the screenplay in particular stands out for its rich detail. The description introduces us to the layout of the ground floor of the house as Cleo simply walks through the spacious rooms while doing her chores:

```
INT - GROUND FLOOR - TEPEJI 21 - DAY

Cleo crosses the dark, antique wood
breakfast room, then the modern light and
angled wood dining room and goes up the
stairs, reaching the hall.

Beyond the hall there are two living rooms,
one with heavy green velvet sofas and
antique cabinets with records and a stereo.
There's a piano next to the wall.

The other living room, with its light sofas
and cocktail tray and siphon attempts to
look more modern.

There's a giant painting in red and purple
hues of a woman leaning on a clay pitcher.

In the other living room, there's another
painting, also large but more somber: In a
dark stone cell, a monk brings solace to a
shackled prisoner who covers his face with
his hands in desperation.
```

What's remarkable about this description is that it is so vivid and specific. We can easily visualize the space, even though it seems to throw a lot of detail at us, through the description of colors and light, of textures and distinctive works of art that populate the home. Not only does the space become real for the reader of the script, but it also reflects the day-to-day lives and interests of this family. The description all by itself tells a story that perhaps even the characters are not fully aware of, but that Cuarón knows intimately. As compared to the way Cuarón used *Roma*'s script as a loose outline for the actors, the way he built the characters' world relied on the script as a very specific tool to make sure that details of set and scenery are "authentic."

Symbolism

One of the most powerful recurring images in the film is that of dog poop. We see the poop from the dog, Borras, prominently in the courtyard and garage, and Señor Antonio even steps in it accidently when leaving his family behind. Most memorably, Señora Sofía yells at Cleo to mop the shit off the garage floor after Señor Antonio drives away, which Cleo does dutifully. The script describes Cleo's cleaning process in detail:

```
EXT - PATIO - TEPEJI 21 - DAY

Cleo pushes the shit onto a dustpan with a
broom.

She moves on to the next one, while Borras
walks around the patio oblivious.

One by one, she picks them all up.

EXT - SMALL PATIO - TEPEJI 21 - DAY

Cleo opens the trash and throws in the
shit. She closes it.

EXT - PATIO - TEPEJI - DAY

A smeared stain on a red and white tile
is all that remains of Borras's shit. Pale
dust falls on the stain until it's entirely
covered.

Cleo crosses the patio, dusting soap on
each one of the remaining stains. She
reaches the street entrance, fills two pails
of water, pours them on the floor and —

One by one, she brushes every single dusted
stain in the patio.
```

DO THE RIGHT THING   FULLER

Why does Cuarón spend so much time describing Cleo cleaning? The symbolism is clear: Cleo is required to literally and figuratively clean up the shit of this family. Clearly, who would want to clean dog poop? But Cleo must — and she does so quietly and methodically. This reflects her role in this family, as well as her attitude toward her role. It's such a powerful scene that is completely original and completely right for this dramatic moment in the aftermath of Señor Antonio abandoning his family and sending the entire household into crisis. Cleo is there to pick up the emotional mess of this family gently, as shown in the way she cleans up the poop.

But in the first instance of the image of dog poop, the mess is already gone. All we see is Cleo at work, and it is only water left to be mopped. Water is used as a symbol in a number of ways throughout the film. First it is a source of cleansing, then a source of joy and danger, and finally of healing at the end of the film at the beach. The water in Cleo's buckets washes the dirt and grime of the house away from the very beginning, and water is most closely associated with her character and role as a caretaker both of the people in the family and the house itself. Ultimately, the water of the sea proves critical to Cleo's development of her own strength. She has shown physical strength before in the narrative, as when she picks up a suitcase of Señor Antonio that is nearly as large as she is, but never physical and emotional courage. And in water she must do so, facing her fear of not being able to swim to save her young charges from drowning. She shows true heroism, seemingly without a second thought. It is a scene that is almost deceptive in its simplicity. And yet, it provides a perfect opportunity for Cleo to expand her already generous heart. We are completely with her when she goes into the sea, walking against huge waves that nearly pull her under but looking straight ahead with such determination that we know she'll save her children — because she considers them hers more than one she could birth on her own.

Roma is a complex film with political references that many Americans will likely not appreciate beyond the surface level. For example, there are references to fighting over land that lead to a fire in the woods near a New Year's celebration party and violent demonstrations during which people are shot and killed. These events live on the periphery of the narrative setting, doing the important work of providing historical context that makes the period depicted more authentic. These details also give life to the world of the film. And yet, at its core, *Roma* is a portrait of a family, a unique microcosm of emotional needs, betrayals, and finally heroism.

In the end, the family heads home from the beach, and things seem to return to normal. Cleo is no longer the grieving guest at the beach, but rather resumes her role as the family caretaker when the younger children ask for banana milkshakes and other snacks. The story has come full circle. But something has changed; every member of the family has been through turmoil. Even the children, the most insulated from the film's conflicts, cry during the trip when Señora Sofía lets them know that their father won't be coming back home. Every member of the family on some level has to decide to move on, to go on, to survive as best they can, but together. Together they find the strength to prevail.

Roma invites us into a world where the hired help is portrayed as both victim and savior, depending on the situation. Dramatic moments big and small make up so much of this film, with issues of race, class, and gender channeled through a character that displays a unique set of emotional and physical skills. Cleo is unforgettable in part because she is an indigenous character who is lifted up and celebrated as the very strong spirit who defies the odds of her lot in life. She fights for her happiness, and while she may not always be self-aware at critical moments, she is always authentically true to herself. A character who is so singularly genuine is one that we might not expect to see in a widely circulated film, but that's the surprise and the delight of this film. We discover what Alfonso Cuarón knew all along: that the people who often get the least consideration in life, who are marginalized, exploited, abandoned by society, are worthy of respect, affection, and dignity.

CHAPTER FIVE

Not So Crazy and Not So Rich Asian Americans

in *ALWAYS BE MY MAYBE* (2019)

"The answers to making it, to me, are a lot more universal than anyone's race or gender, and center on having a tolerance for delayed gratification, a passion for the craft, and a willingness to fail . . . Just accept that you're not a genius. Once I told myself that, I was able to finally write."

— Ali Wong

*A*lways Be My Maybe was ushered into the national conversation through the power of social media. According to *The New Yorker*, "An offhand remark by Ali Wong in a 2016 *New Yorker* article about how she and Randall Park had always wanted to do their version of *When Harry Met Sally* but had never gotten around to it" ignited intense fan interest, leading to demands that the project get made. And "Wong and Park were suddenly swamped with offers for a script that did not exist."[1] Wong previously had a couple of very

---

[1] Jiayang Fan, "What 'Always Be My Maybe' Understands About Making an Asian-American Rom-Com," *The New Yorker*, June 4, 2019, https://www.newyorker.com/culture/cultural-comment/what-always-be-my-maybe-gets-about-making-an-asian-american-rom-com.

successful comedy specials on Netflix — *Baby Cobra* in 2016 and *Hard Knock Wife* in 2018 — while Park was in *Fresh Off the Boat*, the breakthrough Asian American network comedy series on ABC, from 2015 through 2020. (*Fresh Off the Boat* was only the second all-Asian cast sitcom on U.S. network television, after the 1994 sitcom *All American Girl* starring Margaret Cho.)

Always Be My Maybe cowriters and costars Ali Wong and Randall Park came together for the first time through food while Wong was studying at UCLA in the '90s. She entered a fried rice competition that happened to be held at Park's apartment. The party was for members of the LCC Theatre Company, an Asian American comedy and theater group Park cofounded at the university. Wong was an active member at the time, while Park had graduated and was, as Wong says, "a legend" among the group. Even though Park was not aware of Wong at that time, they eventually became friends and frequent collaborators.[2] Ultimately, the two sold the pitch to Netflix. The screenplay that finally resulted from all this fervor, written by Wong, Park, and Michael Golamco, was said in a *New York Times* interview with Wong and Park to have loosely followed

> . . . the structure of *When Harry Met Sally* — a friendship that blooms into love over time, lots of parental involvement, lots of meals. The final version, though, wound up owing nearly as much to another of their favorites, *Boomerang*, the barrier-breaking 1992 comedy about hot black advertising professionals starring Eddie Murphy, Robin Givens and a young Halle Berry as the plain one.[3]

Despite *Boomerang*'s almost completely black cast and story world, race and racism were not dominant issues in the film. This particularly impressed Park, who stated in the same interview, "It was a movie about black people in this elite business world . . . It was just the reality of their lives . . . And I think that spoke to

[2] Alyse Whitney, "Ali Wong and Randall Park on the Real-Life Things That Inspired *Always Be My Maybe*," *Glamour*, June 11, 2019, https://www.glamour.com/story/ali-wong-randall-park-always-be-my-maybe-interview.

[3] Devin Gordon, "What If They Made a Dirty Rom-Com About People Who Looked Like Them?" *The New York Times*, May 28, 2019, https://www.nytimes.com/2019/05/28/movies/always-be-my-maybe.html?smid=em-share.

us."[4] For Wong, the female characters in the film made the greatest impression. She explained that the women "were so strong and weird and eccentric but confident and, like, hot and sexy . . . There's so many different ways women are funny in that movie that you'd never seen before and haven't seen since then."[5]

It might seem strange to characterize the diverting *Always Be My Maybe* as a radical intervention in the history of Asian American film representation in the U.S. There is an old proverb that states "you can catch more flies with honey than with vinegar," meaning it is easier to persuade others with a positive attitude rather than with negativity. In other words, a strong message can be communicated to a broad audience by introducing significant elements of diversity (such as how *Always Be My Maybe* plays with Asian American and African American stereotypes as well as challenges mainstream ideas of class and gender) wrapped in the guise of an unpretentious romantic comedy. A clear focus on character development, and complex and diverse characterizations to introduce these themes, allows the story to be both but remain a coherent whole.

In addition to *When Harry Met Sally* (1989) and *Boomerang* (1992), the writers and stars of *Always Be My Maybe* have specifically named *Notting Hill* (1999) and *Bridget Jones's Diary* (2001) as romantic comedies that inspired them and from which they borrowed select plot devices. For example, both Eddie Murphy's and Randall Park's characters' first names are Marcus, though the characters couldn't have more different individual personalities. Still, while joining the ranks of other rom-coms and staying comfortably within the three-act structure, *Always Be My Maybe* innovates many of the generic conventions significantly, making an often overly predictable narrative fresh.

[4] Gordon, "A Dirty Rom-Com About People Who Looked Like Them."
[5] Gordon, "A Dirty Rom-Com About People Who Looked Like Them."

Conventions of the Romantic Comedy

Rom-com screenplays are usually fairly formulaic: boy meets girl, boy loses girl, boy wins girl back. (It should be noted that rom-coms tend to primarily focus on heterosexual relationships, which clearly reflects the limited diversity of this genre.) The story beats are similarly formulaic, with the following moments the most common in a rom-com script:

- **Introductions:** The audience meets the two main characters separately before those characters meet each other.
- **The meeting moment, aka the "meet cute":** The two characters meet under memorable circumstances, and sparks fly.
- **Falling in love:** The couple's chemistry develops, and their relationship grows.
- **Turning point:** The couple faces a conflict or hurdle, or has an argument that threatens to end their relationship.
- **Breakup:** The couple is (temporarily) torn apart because of their differences.
- **Happy ending:** The couple resolves the conflict, finds true love, and lives happily ever after.[6]

It's clear from the synopsis of *Always Be My Maybe* just how this film plays into — and plays with — these conventions.

Synopsis

Our couple, Sasha Tran and Marcus Kim, meet when they are twelve-year-olds living next door to each other in San Francisco. Sasha is a latchkey kid whose parents work a lot, leaving her alone at home to fend for herself. Marcus invites her over one day and his family welcomes her, especially Marcus' mother Judy, who shares her love of Korean

---

[6] These points are adapted from MasterClass.com: "How to Write A Romantic Comedy Screenplay, Plus 15 Classic Rom-Coms to Watch for Screenwriting Inspiration," accessed February 4, 2022, https://www.masterclass.com/articles/how-to-write-a-romantic-comedy-screenplay-plus-15-classic-rom-coms-to-watch-for-screenwriting-inspiration#what-is-romantic-comedy.

home cooking with Sasha. Fast forward, and now Sasha and Marcus are teenagers who still spend time together hanging out. One day, however, Marcus is with Sasha when he learns that his mother has died in a tragic accident. Afterward, Sasha tries to console a grieving Marcus while in his parked car and then, surprising herself and Marcus, kisses him. They end up having sex in the backseat of the car. Both feel extremely awkward after their encounter and end up fighting in a fast-food restaurant, accusing each other of "acting weird," and split, with their newly intimate relationship unresolved.

Fifteen years pass, with Sasha now a celebrity chef based in Los Angeles and engaged to Brandon Choi, another successful restaurateur. But Brandon is unenthusiastic when Sasha talks about their wedding. He announces travel plans for the next six months and, to add insult to injury, suggests to Sasha that they see other people during that time to be sure of their relationship and marriage. Despite being very hurt, Sasha pretends to be excited about their new plans. Returning to San Francisco to open a new restaurant, Sasha rents a house there. Without Sasha's knowledge, her best friend Veronica arranges for Marcus and his father Harry to come to the house, supposedly to set the air conditioning up but really to try and get Sasha and Marcus romantically back together again. Things are very awkward between them when they meet again. Sasha is underwhelmed with where Marcus is at professionally, especially considering her success as a celebrity chef. Marcus' father even calls her the "Asian Oprah." Marcus, we find out, still lives at home with his dad and plays in a small local band most nights. Before they leave, Harry wistfully says that he always thought Sasha and Marcus would "maybe end up together."

Sasha and Veronica go to see Marcus perform with his band and enjoy themselves. Veronica leaves after the set, but

Marcus' very quirky girlfriend Jenny insists that she cook dinner for Sasha, who she's heard of before. The meal is a disaster to everyone except Jenny, who makes some kind of unappetizing dish using Vienna sausage. When Marcus drives Sasha home, it is in the same car that they lost their virginity in as teenagers. The following day, Brandon calls Sasha and only wants to talk business, so she breaks up with him. Sasha and Marcus start spending more time together, while Harry insists that Sasha is the one for Marcus and that he should tell her how he feels. Just as Marcus is about to admit his romantic feelings for Sasha, she announces that she's ready to start dating again.

While catering a party, Sasha is approached by a man that the audience doesn't see. Sasha then asks Marcus if he and girlfriend Jenny want to have dinner to meet her new man, who turns out to be Keanu Reeves. Sasha and Keanu are all over each other, and Keanu acts in a strange, pretentious manner. Jenny is entranced by Keanu's celebrity, but Marcus is predictably very irritated by him. After dinner, Keanu invites Jenny, Marcus, and Sasha back to his fancy hotel room, where they wind up playing a game similar to "Truth or Dare." In the midst of the game, Sasha confesses that she's had a crush on Marcus her entire life. The game then gets to be an intense competition between Keanu and Marcus, with the two ending up in a physical fight. Sasha is disgusted by Keanu's behavior and leaves with Marcus, while Jenny without hesitation opts to stay with Keanu. During their ride home in an Uber, Sasha and Marcus argue but then begin to make out, and they continue into Sasha's house and bedroom and have sex.

They start dating, with Marcus attending Sasha's red carpet events and Sasha attending Marcus' band gigs, but after a while Marcus gets tired of "holding her purse" at her events. So, when Sasha announces that she will be opening a new restaurant in New York and asks Marcus to join her, though he initially says yes, he really doesn't want to leave his life in San Francisco. Eventually, they argue about her leaving, with Sasha claiming that Marcus is refusing to support her, and finally Marcus admits to her that he doesn't want to go to New York at all. Sasha leaves, crying.

When Marcus returns home, he discovers that his father is dating someone new named Kathy. Shocked, Marcus says that he thought his father needed him to be caretaker after his mother died. But actually, Harry says that he's okay now, it's just Marcus who has been unable to move on. Devastated, Marcus arrives drunk at a gig with his band and pees on the stage. Marcus then realizes that not only has he messed up with his band, but with Sasha as well. He finally moves out of his father's house into his own apartment and works harder to get the band better opportunities in better venues. When Sasha's San Francisco restaurant opens Marcus goes, but Sasha is not there. He looks for Veronica and find boxes of T-shirts in her office that Sasha bough to support Marcus' band from their new website.

Marcus then decides to go to New York to find Sasha at a red carpet event. Once there, he tells her that he loves her and wants to be with her always in front of all the press and guests. She accepts, and Marcus accompanies her as she picks up an award. Afterward, they stop by Sasha's new restaurant, where Marcus is shocked to find out that they are cooking kimchi stew, the Korean dish that his mother used to make, and then sees that Sasha named the restaurant "Judy's Way" in honor of his mother. Sasha says that she wants to make people feel the way Judy made her feel. The story ends with all the characters at the opening of the restaurant.

Playing with Structure

What's truly remarkable about this romantic comedy is that all of the action from the introductions of the couple to the breakup happens in the first ten to fifteen minutes. That's essentially moving through the first five beats of the romantic comedy script (introductions, "meet cute," falling in love, conflict, and breakup) in record time. Notably, however, these first five beats essentially repeat after Marcus and Sasha are reintroduced fifteen years later.

We are reintroduced to the characters, first Sasha as a celebrity chef in Los Angeles, then Marcus, working for his father's air conditioning business in San Francisco. Their second "meet cute" moment at Sasha's rental home in San Francisco is fraught with awkward dialogue: "Long time. Yes. Yes. Very long time, uh, very much so indeed. Uh . . . But, you know, time passes, and now it's like current, modern . . . It's like we're here, and this is great. It's . . ." Marcus falls back in love before, and Sasha after, the disastrous Keanu Reeves double date. The turning point, or conflict, happens over Sasha's planned move to New York. The breakup occurs as she leaves. And the happy ending comes when Marcus follows her to New York and shows up to declare his love.

By repeating the first five story beats, *Always Be My Maybe* allows space for a more complex long-term relationship, with multiple ups and downs. The film still delivers a traditional final beat, the happy ending, with a celebratory kiss on the red carpet, and the audience might initially think that this is the end of the story. However, the complex structure creates more narrative drive and character development that requires an additional moment of resolution beyond the romantic coupling; the first rom-com arc still needs its happy ending. The ending coda, Sasha's reveal of naming her new restaurant after Marcus' mother, is a final defining moment in this film that reaches beyond the typical rom-com ending. It calls back to the opening before Marcus and Sasha fell in love the first time and moves into the realm of healing grief, a reconstituted family and rediscovered cultural heritage. This film tells two stories, one nested inside of the other, and delivers two resolutions instead of one.

Breaking Free of Racial Stereotypes

Marcus' character is staunchly rooted in his working-class identity — a rare acknowledgment in a mainstream film that there are, indeed, class differences in this country. This is humorously brought to our attention through his inappropriate clothing choices on his dates with Sasha. Marcus also smokes weed and plays in a hip-hop band named Hello Peril, a name that might not immediately resonate with most non-Asian viewers. In fact, Hello Peril is a play on the phrase "Yellow Peril," which is a historical racist construct that represents the peoples of East Asia as a threat to Western civilization. That's quite a dark subtext to be included in a straightforward romantic comedy, and just another example of how *Always Be My Maybe* isn't the straightforward romantic comedy that it first appears to be.

Portraying our protagonist Marcus as a weed-smoking dude who heads up a band that plays hip-hop and has no interest in going to college challenges Asian American racial stereotypes head on — he does not fit the stereotypical "model minority" profile that paints a picture of Asian Americans (particularly Asian American men) as nerdy bookworms who do nothing but study for careers in STEM industries and accounting. Yet one might ask why Marcus in the end is compelled to become a more successful musician. Sasha and Marcus' bandmates all confront him at different points in the narrative about his complacency and lack of ambition with Hello Peril. Doesn't he, by changing his approach, adhere to the model minority demand for success in traditional terms? In Marcus' case, fear of success and fear of moving ahead with his life after his mother's death is critical to his character development. This, combined with the fact that a precarious and artistic occupation as a musician (and further still, a musician in a hip-hop band as opposed to, say, a classical pianist) in and of itself works against the typical model minority stereotype, meaning that his goal to improve is more personal and comes across as less generalized.

In another instance of subliminal messaging, Marcus' choice of attire accompanying Sasha at a fancy fundraiser is foreshadowed in the restaurant scene with Keanu Reeves when Marcus, hopelessly overdressed in a tux, is told by Sasha that rich folk habitually underdress by wearing thousand-dollar t-shirts. At the fundraiser, the situation is played for laughs, the humor coming from his sporting a t-shirt among the crowd of tuxedoed men, but the observant viewer will notice that Marcus' t-shirt prominently displays the words "Stay Angry." IndieWire's Hanh Nguyen explains the significance of this seemingly random costume choice in an article about the story behind the t-shirt:

> The shirt and the catchphrase are from Angry Asian Man, whose alter ego is blogger Phil Yu. Since 2001, the Angry Asian Man blog has examined the Asian American experience including news, media, representation, and politics. The site has been a galvanizing force for Asian pride and awareness in the community . . . The annual subscriber fundraiser rewards donors with a custom-designed T-shirt that reads "Stay Angry" to remind readers to not settle for the status quo.[7]

Clearly, every opportunity was taken by the filmmakers to create layers of meaning for different audiences without sacrificing entertaining content.

Sasha's career as a celebrity chef also pushes back against the myth that Asian Americans lack creativity and individualism or that they are all essentially cut from the same mold. Not only does her profession majorly distinguish her as a fascinating personality, her costuming, foregrounded as alternately artistic and glamorous — basically, just very cool — reinforces this. Further, Sasha's character shatters the submissive Asian female stereotype so prevalent in Western films. She is assertive, with a keen wit, from the time we first meet her as a twelve-year-old to the moment when she breaks up

---

[7] Hanh Nguyen, "'Always Be My Maybe': Here's the Story Behind That 'Stay Angry' T-Shirt," IndieWire, June 1, 2019, https://www.indiewire.com/2019/06/always-be-my-maybe-stay-angry-asian-man-t-shirt-netflix-1202146399/.

with her restaurateur boyfriend, Brandon, loudly cursing at him and disrupting an entire birthday celebration. She speaks her mind always, whether she's describing her night of sex with Keanu Reeves to Marcus or insisting that Marcus support her career and lifestyle or else end their relationship.

Sasha's feminist leanings run very much counter to the female characterization found in some of the romantic comedies that served as influences for *Always Be My Maybe*. For example, Anna, the actress from *Notting Hill*, gives up a world-class career for marriage and a family (the movie ends with a prominent pregnancy), and the persistent loneliness the character Bridget Jones displays is by far her most defining trait. That loneliness is also the most relevant to Sasha's predicament. However, unlike the very successful Sasha, Bridget is shown as both incompetent and unprofessional in all her work situations. Bridget is presented as a "charmingly imperfect" character who only the right man can help make whole by "accepting her as she is." And in the film *When Harry Met Sally*, all Harry and Sally talk about as a couple, first and foremost, are romantic relationships, overwhelmingly situated as the most compelling topic for both main and supporting characters throughout the world of the film.

The film *Boomerang* is notable for the way the two female characters who vie for Marcus' attention and affection, Jacqueline and Angela, are both introduced as successful in their respective professions. Jacqueline is Marcus' new boss, while Angela is a quieter but always professional staffer. Still, the ending subtly but noticeably presents the traditional view of an artificial binary of success at work versus a happy romantic life for women characters; significantly, Angela is promoted and becomes (unhappily) more work focused after she breaks up with Marcus. Her unhappiness in this film, as with the others, indicates that a woman needs to choose between professional success and personal happiness. It's still not the norm in the rom-com genre that the woman in the heterosexual couple could be more successful, as Sasha is in *Always Be My Maybe* — or more importantly that, if she is more successful, she doesn't have to sacrifice her success to win the man.

Asian Americans Are Americans, Not Foreigners

Asian American characters are still often depicted as having accents, but not in this movie! Instead, the primary cultural distinction through Asian food is significant because it nourishes and sustains all of the characters without language, and without obscuring their shared American national identity. Clearly, food functions as a cultural touchstone in this film, especially since Sasha's job is as a chef.

Additionally, there is strong association with African American music. In fact, the music we first hear in the film's opening title sequence and throughout is primarily hip-hop. The title of the film is a play on the Mariah Carey hit song "Always Be My Baby," which is finally heard over the end credits sequence. David Bowie's song "Young Americans," meanwhile, is played over the montage of Marcus and Sasha growing up, aurally reinforcing their American identity.

The choice of Keanu Reeves as a love interest is another subtle but intentional inclusion that would resonate with an Asian American audience on multiple levels. Keanu's appearance in the film is explained in an IndieWire article by Hanh Nguyen:

> The Asian American community . . . never forgets that he's also part Chinese-Hawaiian and claims him as one of their own. It's that blend of global megastar name recognition and Asian identification that makes him the perfect choice to send up in . . . *Always Be My Maybe*.[8]

Keanu Reeves is a mainstream star who is comically integrated in the action against his usual action hero type of films like *The Matrix* and *John Wick*. It seems that every character, not just the protagonists, is working to redefine what it means to be Asian American.

---

[8] Hanh Nguyen, "How 'Always Be My Maybe' Got Keanu Reeves to Jab at His Own Mystique Through a Love Story," IndieWire, June 3, 2019, https://www.indiewire.com/2019/06/keanu-reeves-always-be-my-maybe-i-punched-keanu-reeves-netflix-1202146517/.

Keanu Reeves as a plot device goes above and beyond the cameo appearance in *Notting Hill* of Alec Baldwin as Anna's current boyfriend making a surprise visit to London, which clearly inspired it.

Quirky and Multidimensional Characters

Marcus' quirky Asian American girlfriend Jenny wears her hair in dreadlocks, an obvious association with African American physicality and culture that is played for laughs. Remarkably, the usual plot device of a romantic triangle is not played out between Sasha, Jenny, and Marcus. Such a love triangle is exemplified in *Bridget Jones's Diary*, with Bridget completely consumed by her decision to choose either boss Daniel Cleaver (Hugh Grant) or Mark Darcy (Colin Firth) for a romantic relationship. In *Always Be My Maybe*, instead of the two women being portrayed as angry or desperate for Marcus' affection, they actually seem to get along rather well and don't view each other as competitors (Jenny voices her admiration for Sasha's stellar career as a chef). The more predictable route is taken between Marcus and Keanu Reeves getting into a physical fight over Sasha, which directly parallels the fight between Daniel Cleaver and Mark Darcy over Bridget, but unlike in *Bridget Jones's Diary*, this fight doesn't represent a climactic moment for either Marcus or Sasha.

Even the supporting character of Marcus' father Harry Kim has a story arc that defies prior caricatured depictions of older Asian men as solely paternal and asexual. At a birthday party in one scene, Harry shows a seemingly passing interest in a young and attractive African American Diana Ross impersonator that is initially played for laughs. However, in a surprising reveal late in the film, Marcus catches his Dad making out with her in his house. But instead of the bit becoming a cheap gag, Harry explains to Marcus in a very key, if brief, scene that he has moved on, and that Marcus should too. Harry then ends the scene with a gesture protective of his new partner that is as much touching as it is humorous, saying to Marcus, "And please, don't be a downer in front of Kathy." Her character is not only given a name, she is given respect and consideration. And she also appears in the final scene at the opening of Sasha's New York restaurant, sitting next to Harry. They are clearly a real couple. Harry's seemingly small gesture takes on more weight when Marcus stops by their booth and asks his Dad gently, "Do you think Mom would have liked this?" Harry responds in kind — "I think she would have loved it" — as Kathy looks on unobtrusively, but she isn't being sidelined; she's giving the father and son their moment of resolution, that same respect that was shown to her.

Inclusion of Tragedy and Resilience

The loss of Marcus' mother, Judy Kim, comes very early in the story. In fact, Marcus finds out that there's been an accident involving his mom when he is teaching Sasha how to fish for the first time when they are teens. The switch in tone from lighthearted to tragic is swift, but somehow seems organic both to the core of who these characters are as well as the story that is being told. The scene of the wake is brief but telling, as Marcus' father Harry frantically looks for coffee filters in the kitchen cabinets so that he can prepare coffee for their many guests and Marcus states that he didn't "know where she [Judy] kept them."

The story is not afraid to delve into issues of loneliness, showing a young Sasha preparing her dinner and eating alone in front of the TV in the very first scene of the film. This scene is echoed once Sasha returns to San Francisco fifteen years later as a successful chef; this time her meal has a gourmet touch, but she is still all by herself. The scenes of Sasha as a lonely child and then a lonely adult resonate very differently than Bridget Jones' drunken rendition of the song "All by Myself" when first we meet her. Sasha's loneliness is more profound and longstanding rather than framed as stemming from any lack in herself.

While the loss of a parent in a romance is not uncommon, truly diving in and exploring the unaddressed grief that follows seems rather heavy, particularly for a romantic comedy, in which the usual conflict is between a couple and a rival rather than originating in the deep emotional wounds that need to be healed within each individual. And yet, this effectively creates a palpable vulnerability in both Marcus and Sasha.

True Love, Not Romance

Netflix's podcast "Watching With . . ." presented an episode on *Always Be My Maybe* featuring director Nahnatchka Khan and co-writer and star Randall Park in which the significance of ending the film differently from most conventional romantic comedies is addressed. While the finale certainly delivers on a dramatic and glamorous romantic kiss, Sasha and Marcus together on the red carpet with lightbulbs flashing, the kiss, as host Jarett Wieselman opines, "isn't the whole point of the movie." Director Nahnatchka Khan agrees: "That's not our movie."[9] Her statement was quite possibly a reference to the hit Asian American film *Crazy Rich Asians* released the year before.

By definition, a plot twist disrupts what the audience thinks they already know or already have figured out. It creates a change in direction for the expected outcome. As discussed when exploring the nested story structure, the true resolution comes in the scene that follows the big kiss. It's a very quiet, intimate scene leading to the big reveal for Marcus and the audience of Sasha's unpretentious new restaurant, Judy's Way, and its menu. Far from abandoning her career for personal happiness, this story's resolution generously serves both Marcus and Sasha equally. This final career move shows Sasha providing both a loving gesture to Marcus and reaching her own emotional and professional fulfillment, taking the plot full circle, from the primary loss of a family member to a reconstituted family. It's a deeper statement on the nature of the kind of love that goes beyond simply a romantic couple into understanding the essential need for family and home. In fact, Sasha says exactly this in the scene: "This is what I want to do, Marcus. The kind of food

---

[9] "Always Be My Maybe with Nahnatchka Khan and Randall Park," *Watching With...* Podcast audio, July 3, 2019, https://podcasts.apple.com/tz/podcast/always-be-my-maybe-with-nahnatchka-khan-and-randall-park/id1464225558?i=1000443544992.

that makes people feel at home. The way your mom always made me feel."

Always Be My Maybe tackles some rather heavy subject matter — sometimes head on, sometimes through subtle choices, but always with the light touch of a romantic comedy. And in doing so, through the range of themes and plot devices discussed here, the film avoids the generic story clichés. Themes such as career, love, loss, family, and culture combine to produce a unique take on a well-worn though still-popular genre. While Sasha doesn't want to be (or feel) alone and Marcus is afraid to move ahead with his life, both change for the better in the end. And in the end, *Always Be My Maybe*'s greatest achievement might be that it showcases the talent and highlights the lived experience of Asian Americans, which gives us hope that we too, as well as the larger society, can shift to a more inclusive and diverse one.

Get
to
Work

on the Screenplay
Only You Can Write

*"I would say, as a black filmmaker, it's easy for me to focus
my attention on black work, but true change would include brown
work, and it would include work by Asian Americans, and it
would include natives, and it would include women, and it would
include more LGBTQ voices."*

— Ava DuVernay

We began this book with a recognition that the film industry was changing and a declaration that more diversity, equity, and inclusivity is necessary in film, particularly in screenwriting. Screenwriting is at the heart of every film because it's where the story starts. It's the blueprint from which everything else originates. The importance of telling diverse stories — stories that have not been told before, stories that only we can tell — cannot be stated often enough. This book is meant to encourage and inspire screenwriters to try different genres as well as different perspectives, with an emphasis on collaboration. Hopefully, reading about the five screenplays included in this book that embrace diversity in significant ways will be useful for your own writing. I consider these screenplays as case studies to review for differences in form and approach that can be referenced or can simply inspire.

More than one of the writers of these screenplays is quoted as expecting no one to be interested in the story they set out to tell. Hard to believe, given the extraordinary quality of the work. But guess what? In spite of that belief, they did it anyway. They persevered with their unique vision, their special take on the human condition — a take sometimes so personal that it seemed to the screenwriter they would have no audience other than themselves and *possibly* their loved ones. I chose these quotes for a reason: to hopefully show how even established filmmakers have serious doubts about their story ideas, especially if they're introducing something new and different from what's come before.

It's hard to put yourself and your work out there, and it always will be. But imagine a world without the screenplays and films included in this book. The world needs more and different stories. The world needs *your* stories. As competitive as the industry is, why are good stories so hard to come by? In part, because the same few people, or the same "type" of people, are writing the scripts. By "type," I don't mean a particular demographic, but rather a mindset that privileges safe subjects over something new, even if the resulting films are clichéd, formulaic, stereotypical, or derivative, and have essentially been done a hundred times before. And yet, audiences are clamoring for new stories that reflect their real lived experiences.

Be the screenwriter to take a chance and to take a creative risk. There are so many different kinds of stories to adapt and make your own. There are original stories in your head just waiting for you to manifest them on paper or screen or index cards or whatever the case may be. Write whatever excites or inspires you or makes you sad, what moves you emotionally in some significant way. Try romantic comedies, thrillers, historical dramas (sound familiar?). Between adaptation and original ideas, you can start a screenplay that, like the films featured in this book, explores the depth of characters, layers your stories with the nuances of intersectionality, and reflects experiences that no one has ever seen featured on screen before. That is my hope. So write on!

ABOUT THE AUTHOR

KARLA RAE FULLER, MFA, PhD, is currently an Associate Professor in the department of Cinema and Television Arts at Columbia College Chicago, where she teaches Cinema Studies and Screenwriting to undergraduates and MFA students. She received her PhD from Northwestern University, MFA from Columbia University in New York City, and BA from Amherst College.

Prior to teaching at Columbia College, Fuller held the position of Director of Feature Film Evaluation at Vestron Inc., which produced the hit movie *Dirty Dancing*. She was also a freelance script reader for New Line Cinema, Miramax, and other production companies.

Her research interests include racial and ethnic representation in Hollywood films, postwar Japanese cinema, and authorship studies. She has presented her work at film and media conferences both nationally and internationally and published in numerous film journals. Fuller has published an essay in the anthology *Classic Hollywood, Classic Whiteness* on the representation of the Japanese in Hollywood films during World War II.

Her book *Hollywood Goes Oriental: CaucAsian Performance in American Film* was released by Wayne State University Press in 2010. She edited and introduced *Ang Lee: Interviews*, a compilation of interviews of award-winning director Ang Lee published by the University Press of Mississippi in 2016, with Korean and Chinese translations published in 2019 and 2022, respectively.

© MICHELE MONTEZ

MICHAEL WIESE PRODUCTIONS

I N A DARK TIME, a light bringer came along, leading the curious and the frustrated to clarity and empowerment. It took the well-guarded secrets out of the hands of the few and made them available to all. It spread a spirit of openness and creative freedom, and built a storehouse of knowledge dedicated to the betterment of the arts.

The essence of Michael Wiese Productions (MWP) is empowering people who have the burning desire to express themselves creatively. We help them realize their dreams by putting the tools in their hands. We demystify the sometimes secretive worlds of screenwriting, directing, acting, producing, film financing, and other media crafts.

By doing so, we hope to bring forth a realization of 'conscious media,' which we define as being positively charged, emphasizing hope, and affirming positive values like trust, cooperation, self-empowerment, freedom, and love. Grounded in the deep roots of myth, it aims to be healing both for those who make the art and those who encounter it. It hopes to be transformative for people, opening doors to new possibilities and pulling back veils to reveal hidden worlds.

MWP has built a storehouse of knowledge unequaled in the world, for no other publisher has so many titles on the media arts. Please visit www.mwp.com, where you will find many free resources and a 25% discount on our books. Sign up and become part of the wider creative community!

MICHAEL WIESE, Co-Publisher
GERALDINE OVERTON, Co-Publisher

CPSIA information can be obtained
at www.ICGtesting.com
Printed in the USA
JSHW042256100822
28749JS00002BA/2

9 781615 933402